*The Phoenix Hecht*

# Treasury Manager's

# Bookmarks and Favorite Places

For information, contact:
Phoenix-Hecht
PO Box 13628, 68 TW Alexander Drive
Research Triangle Park, NC 27709

ISBN: 0-9654739-1-0

# TABLE OF CONTENTS

# PREFACE

Presently, the Internet represents a small but rapidly growing body of knowledge for treasury managers. Service providers are continually evaluating their web site strategy with the expectations of generating revenue. As a result, the Internet is in a constant state of flux. This project is our second attempt to bring some order to the chaos of cyberspace. The purpose of this project is to share our findings of Internet searches for useful treasury information. The intent is to save you valuable time and effort when you need to use the resources of the Internet. Since many of the sites indexed in this guide are evolving, we expect that some of the pages may look different than the illustrations and that even the Uniform Resource Locators may change. The Phoenix-Hecht web site (http://www.phoenixhecht.com), however, will have the most current links.

This effort never could have been possible without the support of the following industry providers who, like us, believed in the value of the project.

ABN AMRO/LaSalle National Bank
AmSouth Bank
Bank of New York
Ernst & Young
First Union National Bank
Mellon Bank
NationsBank
PNC Bank
Provident Bank
SunGard Treasury Systems
SunTrust Banks
UMB Banks
Union Bank of California
Wachovia Bank

David A. Bochnovic
Executive Vice President
Phoenix-Hecht

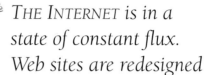 *THE INTERNET is in a state of constant flux. Web sites are redesigned daily, updated hourly. That is, after all, the beauty of the Web. Many of the sites mentioned in this guide are evolving. We anticipate that some of the sites you visit as a result of using this guide may look different than depicted in the illustrations and that new editorial features may have been added to these sites. Our purpose in publishing this guide is to steer you to sites of value and to encourage you to visit your favorite sites with some frequency. You will certainly see changes and improvements at these sites which will enhance the time you spend on the Internet.*

# INTRODUCTION

Our purpose in publishing this index is to provide you with a more targeted entry point to the Web for treasury management related information. Finding relevant information on the Internet for a treasury manager was no easy feat. Over 1,000 man hours were spent using multiple search engines just to compile the sites and web pages reviewed in this book. We recognized that no treasury manager would individually invest that much time searching for such a specialized body of knowledge. One of the biggest problems with web searches is they can consume an inordinate amount of time relative to the amount of useable information found.

## Why do searches consume so much valuable time?

For the most part search engines rely on databases maintained by the search engine companies. Owners of a site embed keywords in their site registration which draw the attention of the search engine. Clever web site designers frequently overload these registrations with multiple key words or a single key word repeated an excessive number of times. The more key words found, the greater the probability of a "hit" by a search engine. This is also why many searches return multiple listings of the same site. Of course, search technology is constantly being refined, but, until it is further refined, a pair of human eyes is still the best judge of value.

In indexing the sites described in this book, Phoenix-Hecht employed multiple search engines and examined each and every returned listing. Specifically, we were looking for pages that contained the requested information rather than just more links. Some of the sites we found provided a wealth of information for different treasury management disciplines. Descriptions or listings for each of these sites may be found under the appropriate topic heading. We wrote descriptions of the site features which we thought had educational value rather than just duplicating a company brochure.

Our original publication, *The Treasury Manager's Guide to the Internet,* dealt with web sites organized by type of organization, i.e, bank, association, government, etc. At the time, we felt that this was the best way for a treasury manager to relate to what was available on the Web.

In this publication, we have organized the web pages based on a treasury management topic. In some instances, we have highlighted specific pages from a service provider in an effort to save you the additional task of "constant clicking" when starting from a home page.

## What has changed?

Sometimes it is hard to believe the graphical user interface web portion of the Internet has only been in existence since 1993. Since that time, the Web has moved from a novelty into a full scale business tool. In a recent Phoenix-Hecht survey, 80% of corporate treasury managers reported having Internet access from their desktop at work. At the time of the survey, corporate treasury use of the Internet was primarily e-mail to communicate with vendors, suppliers and bankers.

While the Web has grown faster than any other communication device in history, this is mostly a consumer driven phenomenon. Initial bank offerings have focused on providing retail services as a way to reduce distribution costs. Web site development by providers of treasury management services currently lag the retail consumer development efforts from these providers. The corporate treasury side of the Web is still in a primitive state but is evolving daily. The majority of service provider sites we examined lack inter-activity and intimate details of product services. We did not find many service sites providing technical data such as service agreements, product specifications or pricing which could aid you in a purchasing decision.

Many of the web-based applications a treasury manager might use, such as receiving bank statements, are only accessible to bank customers. This book does not address comparisons of these services, but rather focuses on the web sites which provide information to customers and prospects alike.

The most significant change to the Web since our last evaluation of the Internet, is the growing number of restricted or fee-based web sites. Information providers see the Internet as a delivery mechanism to produce revenue from their content. Timeliness, accessibility and demand for the information is the key to getting this business model to work. Yet this business model in not widely accepted by the Web user. For example, you can read almost every major newspaper without having to subscribe.

Having access to the Internet is similar to having a library card. The card permits access to the library at any time of the day or night. But having access is only half the battle. The treasury manager's use of the Internet does not come without a cost. Unfortunately, even the best search engines return thousands of erroneous findings. The Internet does not recognize that the amount of time you, as a treasury manager, can spare is limited. Certainly research tasks can be assigned to a staff member provided you have outlined a specific query, but even then a considerable amount of time will be spent on-line. By utilizing this book our hope is that you will save time.

## What's out there?

For treasury managers, the most attractive portion of the Internet, besides e-mail, is the ability to do research and access a vast array of information sources on the World Wide Web. The treasury function at most corporations has to deal with a wide variety of subjects of which no one individual can be completely knowledgeable. The Internet can be an excellent vehicle to stay abreast of many subjects. Fortunately, many of the vendors servicing the corporate treasury area have portions of their web site where access to this information is free.

In our original research, we categorized and selected web sites based on their value to treasury managers. In this project we also considered sites to include which had the following attributes:

**Data Warehouse Sites:** Data warehouse sites contain data such as current or historical interest rates for different securities, foreign exchange rates, Federal Reserve data or stock quotes. There may be a monthly fee for some data warehouse sites.

**Content Sites:** Content sites make available newsletters, economic forecasts, articles, position papers or other material previously published in other sources. The better content sites have a search engine at their site to make navigation quicker.

**Catalog Sites:** Catalog sites are the most common of web sites. Catalog web pages describe the provider's product or service. They are similar in content to a product or company brochure. Catalog sites are evolving to include recent press releases, financial information, names and contact information on key personnel in sales and customer service.

**Transactional Sites:** Transactional sites are the holy grail of the Internet. These are sites where you can conduct e-commerce for goods or services. Many of the Internet's transactional sites are electronic extensions of a conventional business.

**Forum Sites:** Forum sites are interactive sites that solicit user questions and post the responses for others to view. These sites function much like a town meeting to address issues.

**Index Sites:** Index sites are web sites which track the information on other sites by providing a description or editorial on the content available. This book, and the corresponding web site from Phoenix-Hecht, is arranged as a large easy-to-navigate index site.

As part of our review process, we selectively picked web sites of value to the treasury manager. From this unique group we awarded sites a rating of up to four stars based on how much content value the site would have for a treasury manager. The more original material or comprehensive and well organized links to the relevant sites, the higher the rating. These ratings are not an endorsement of any provider, but rather simply another method to help you save time in your search for information on the Web.

The uniqueness of the Internet is evidenced by not only the different categories of sites but also by what information the different providers have elected to make available and at what cost. The key to using the Internet is to effectively find the sites which work for you. Our goal in the book is to make your search more efficient, more effective and more fun.

If you're still filing your paid checks, tracking down an old check is like looking for a needle in a haystack. But with Union Bank of California's innovative CLEAR/IMAGE Hindsight℠ service, you can easily find any stored check in seconds. Just give us your old checks and we'll convert them to CDs. Up to 20,000 images can be stored on each CD. And they can be accessed by check number, amount, or date. For the fastest way to find your stored checks, call today. Your search has ended.

# You have *five* minutes to find check #3067, dated March 18, 1993. *Go.*

UNION
BANK OF
CALIFORNIA ℠

# CHAPTER 1

# Capital Markets

*SHORT-TERM INVESTMENTS and
borrowing are driven by the
available rates in the market
for these products and services.
Likewise, long-term rates in
the debt and equity markets
determine the cost of capital for
an organization. This section
provides sites which offer
information to the treasurer
on various rates for different
segments of the market.* ▟

For cash management purposes, the short-term side of the market is of most interest. For a company with surplus funds there are a variety of different investment options ranging from savings-type accounts at banks to commercial paper to high-risk derivative-type investments. Those in charge of their organization's short-term investments should make sure they have a current statement of investment policy which outlines the investments and levels, as well as risk profiles, that are acceptable to senior management.

Traditionally, most short-term borrowing has been provided by commercial banks, but more and more companies are using non-bank sources of credit and direct placements such as commercial paper for their borrowing needs. Base rates for short-term borrowing are usually driven by the Prime rate (the best rate offered by large commercial banks for unsecured loans), and more often today, LIBOR (London InterBank Offer Rate), which are then adjusted to reflect the riskiness of the borrower. Many companies also utilize some type of secured borrowing, using assets such as accounts receivable or inventory to back their loan or to provide basic financing for that asset.

On the long-term side, treasurers must be concerned with the rates on intermediate and long-term loans and bonds issues, as well as the cost of equity financing. Cost of capital for any given company or organization is generally driven by a large number of factors. These factors are often market-related or specific to the firm, but may also be driven by economic or industry trends. Regardless, the treasurer must keep abreast of developments in capital markets and the various rates which can impact the ultimate profitability of the organization.

## Descriptions of Money Market Investments

http://www.moneymarkets.com/reference.html

## Daily Rates

http://www.ny.frb.org/pihome/mktrates/

The Federal Reserve Bank of New York provides one of the better sites for daily rates on commercial paper (CP) and foreign exchange (FX). Daily rates are available for dealer-placed and direct-placed commercial paper plus 36 foreign currencies. These are the noon buying rates "as certified by the New York Federal Reserve Bank for customs purposes." All of the rates shown are expressed in terms of foreign currency values (e.g., currently 135.26 yen/dollar) except for U.K. Sterling rates which are shown in terms of U.S. dollars per pound. In addition, you can access the New York Federal Reserve's 10:00 a.m. midpoint (between buying and selling rates) foreign exchange rates daily for major currencies expressed in foreign currency units:

> Pound Sterling
> (expressed in US$ equivalents)
> Canadian Dollar
> French Franc
> German Mark
> Swiss Franc
> Japanese Yen
> Dutch Guilder
> Belgian Franc
> Italian Lira
> Swedish Krone
> Norwegian Krone
> Danish Krone

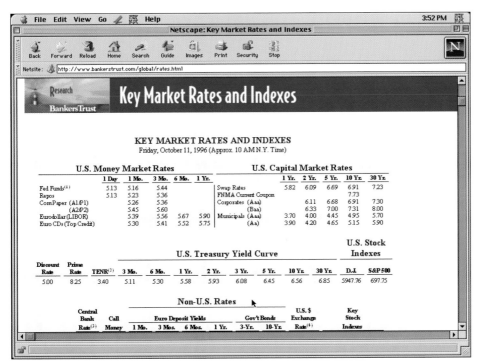

*Bankers Trust's Key Market Interest Rates*

## Key Market Interest Rates provided by Bankers Trust

http://www.bankerstrust.com/global/rates.html

## Commercial Paper Rates and Outstandings

http://www.bog.frb.fed.us/releases/CP/

A Federal Reserve Board release of commercial paper rates derived from data supplied by The Depository Trust Company.

*Federal Reserve Board Commercial Paper Rates*

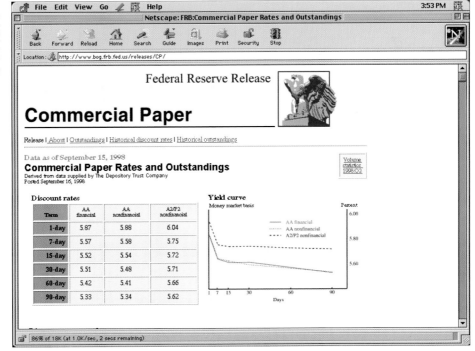

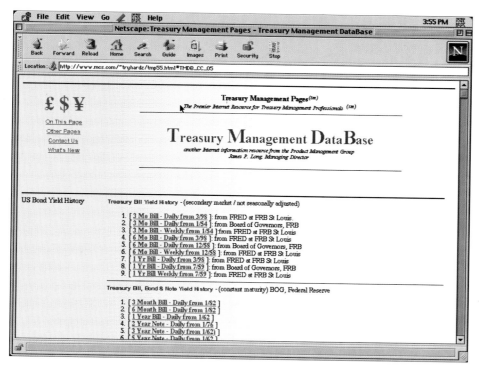

*James P. Long's Treasury Management Index Site*

## Bankers Acceptances and Commercial Paper Rates

http://www.mcs.com/~tryhardz/tmp55.html
#TMDB_CC_05

Not all of the published rates by the Federal Reserve are well organized. This site organizes links to the specific Federal Reserve Releases provided as part of the Treasury Management DataBase, an Internet information resource from the Product Management Group and James P. Long, Managing Director.

## Money Market Rates

http://www.moneymarkets.com/

This site, dedicated to cash management and money market investments, maintains postings of money market investment instruments offering interactive dealing in fixed income securities. Access fee required for some quotations. A private web page can be established for you to list your portfolio of securities.

## Interest Rates

http://www.bog.frb.fed.us/Releases/H15/update/

*Federal Reserve Board Statistics: Current Interest Rates and Historical Data*

The weekly release is posted on Monday. Daily updates of the weekly release are posted Tuesday through Friday on this site.

## Historical Interest Rates

http://www.stls.frb.org/fred/indx.html

FRED provides historical U.S. economic and financial data, including daily U.S. interest rates, monetary and business indicators, exchange rates, and regional economic data. FRED files are grouped into twelve categories:

Daily/Weekly U.S. Financial Data
Monthly Monetary Data
Monthly Interest Rates
Monthly Reserves
Monthly Commercial Banking Data

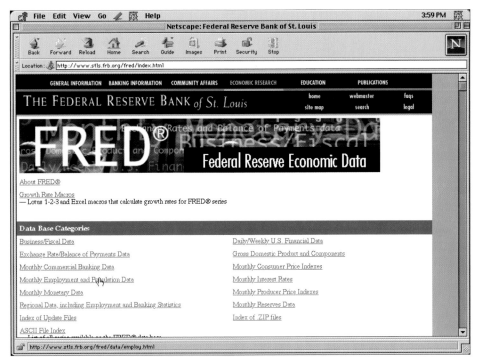

*Federal Reserve Economic Data*

Business/Fiscal Data
Gross Domestic Product and Components
Monthly Consumer Price Indexes
Monthly Producer Price Indexes
Monthly Employment and Population Data
Exchange Rate and Balance of
    Payments Data
Monthly Regional Data

You can download data from FRED databases in ASCII format for use in other programs. Or you can use a new feature that allows you to request that data be downloaded and sent to you via e-mail. If you are looking for historic financial data, FRED should be your starting point.

## Short-Term Investment Practices

http://www.treasurystrat.com/tsi/
download.html

The annual Liquidity Management Survey from the consulting firm Treasury Strategies measures the short-term investment practices of corporations. The survey looks at the use of investment instruments, distribution channels, maturity structure and time spent managing investments. Survey respondents are given a free Executive Summary of Findings and a customized individual benchmark report.

## Municipal Bonds

http://www.tradehistory.com

Trading information and price comparisons for municipal and some corporate and convertible bonds are provided by Trade History LLC. Registration is required.

## Money Market Mutual Fund Data

http://www.ibcdata.com/bradshaw/
topcds.htm

IBC Financial Data is known for its publications, *IBC's Money Fund Report, IBC's Money Market Insight, IBC's Rated Money Fund Report, IBC's Money Fund Expense*

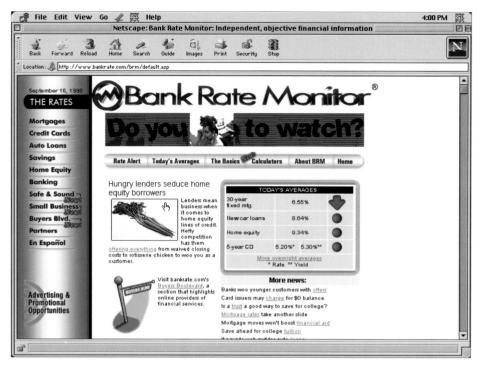

*Bank Rate Monitor*

Report, and the **Bradshaw Financial Network's RateGram**. Most require a subscription. This site provides some CD and MMDA yields.

## Commercial Borrowing, Lending and Loan Syndications
### Gold Sheets On-line

http://www.loanpricing.com/gs.htm

Gold Sheets On-Line is Loan Pricing Corporation's weekly publication of commercial borrowing, lending and loan syndications detailing the most comprehensive loan market news and analysis available. There is information on syndicated loan market trends in most major industries, tables that rank bank lenders, feature stories, who's borrowing and searchable indexes. LPC is a Reuters company.

## Bank Rates for mortgages, credit cards, auto loans

http://www.bankrate.com/brm/default.asp

Bank Rate Monitor provides more than 1,600 pages of free rates for mortgages, home equity loans, savings, new and used auto loans, credit cards and checking accounts via the Internet. Bank Rate Monitor also tracks retail ATM and checking account fees and on-line banking fees. More than 2,500 institutions are surveyed weekly. The database is updated nightly Monday through Friday.

## Terms of Business Lending
### Fed Survey

http://www.bog.frb.fed.us/Releases/E2/

These data are collected during the middle month of each quarter and are released in the middle of the succeeding month. The files are available in Adobe Acrobat™ portable document format (PDF) only.

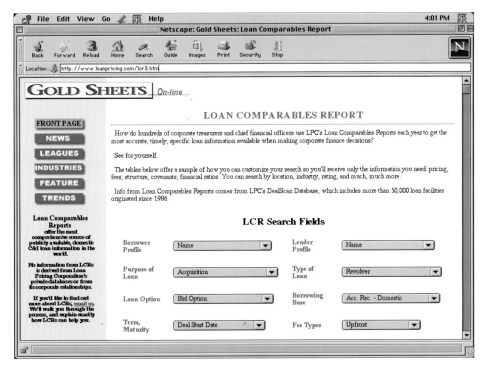

*Loan Pricing Corporation's loan analysis*

## Loan Comparables Report ☆☆☆

http://www.loanpricing.com/lcr3.htm

Loan Comparables Report offers a comprehensive source of publicly available, domestic C&I loan information. No information is derived from Loan Pricing Corporation's private databases or from its corporate relationships.

# Where are you?

Has rightsizing left you with fewer resources in a more competitive market?

## Does it seem like your workload is rising faster than your bottom line?

We are here. To offer practical solutions that enhance productivity and convert workflow into cash flow. To provide the right technology for managing your treasury, trust and investment information in more effective ways. To streamline or even take on the time-consuming tasks related to collections, payments and benefits. And to deliver the quality and reliability that turns your productivity into profits. Talk to us.

## We are here.

**WACHOVIA**

1-800-422-4950
WWW.WACHOVIA.COM

Let's get started.

## CHAPTER 2

# Cash Management

*THE CASH MANAGEMENT AREA of a corporation is often defined in terms of managing short-term assets and liabilities. This section of **The Internet Index** deals with the day-to-day cash management tasks focusing on the collection, concentration and disbursement of the company's cash.*

The cash management area of an organization is often defined in terms of managing the short-term assets and liabilities of that organization. While this section focuses on general cash management topics, several of the sections below provide more detail on specific areas of cash management. Many of the day-to-day cash management tasks focus on the collection, concentration and disbursement of cash for an organization. Commercial banks provide many of the services used in the cash management area for accomplishing these day-to-day cash management functions.

On the collection side, there are many bank and a few non-bank providers of lockbox and other collection services for cash managers. These services are typically used to speed up the collection of checks and other types of payments so that the organization can receive available funds as quickly as possible. The cash management collection phase is actually at the very end of the accounts receivable or credit cycle for a company, and typically starts when the customer puts the check in the mail in payment for goods and/or services. The job of the cash manager is to transform that "check in the mail" into available funds as quickly as possible.

The concentration portion of the cash management responsibility is concerned with moving funds received at remote collection points (often stores in a retail entity or perhaps lockboxes) into a central point for use by the company. Where there are large dollar amounts involved (as in a wholesale corporate lockbox), the speed of the concentration method becomes important due to the time value of money and wires may be used to move these funds. Where there are a large number of small dollar transfers involved (as in a chain of retail stores), reducing transaction costs related to the concentration efforts becomes more important and ACH may be used to move the funds.

The disbursement area of cash management is primarily focused on timing and control. In disbursing funds, an organization will want to consider all available discounts for early payment as well as making best use of any credit terms offered by suppliers. The issue of whether to manage payables and disbursements on a centralized or decentralized basis must also be considered.

Other treasury-related topics such as accounts payable and receivable management, electronic commerce, international treasury, risk management and pension management are each detailed in following chapters.

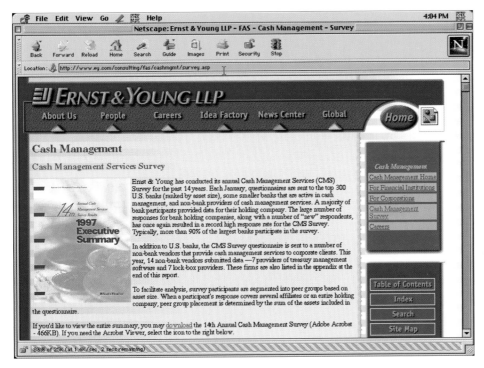

Ernst & Young's annual cash management survey

## Cash and Treasury Management Industry Calendars

Most treasury management publications offer some type of calendar of events. While no one vendor appears to have the most complete listing of conferences, three stand out with extensive listings or multiple year date books.

### Treasury Management Association
http://www.tma-net.org/confeduc/calendar.html

### Phoenix-Hecht
http://www.phoenixhecht.com/calendar

### Business Finance Magazine
http://www.businessfinancemag.com/index.html?CMRD=Y

## Cash Management Basics
http://www.patterson.net/arti-003.html#mgmtview

An article for smaller companies on cash management but contains good fundamentals.

## Cash Management in Commercial Banking
http://www.ey.com/consulting/fas/cashmgmt/survey.asp

Ernst & Young reveals the key findings of their annual cash management services survey, in which a majority of the largest U.S. banks participated. An Adobe Acrobat™ Viewer is required to view the downloaded file. The E&Y site contains a number of special industry reports from their different consulting specialties. A site search engine is provided.

In 1998, it is rare to find a bank that does not have some kind of presence on the Internet, and the general usefulness of many large commercial bank sites has increased significantly in the last few years. However, most bank sites are still retail-oriented with limited offerings for the commercial customer. One area that has shown significant improvement is the availability of on-line banking for small business customers through the use of products such as Quicken for Business and QuickBooks.

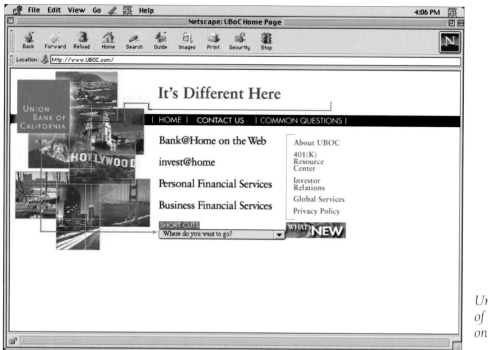

*Union Bank
of California
on-line banking*

One good aspect of the Internet is that it allows a treasury manager to easily survey the different offerings available from the banks in the marketplace. This is especially valuable as more and more banks are merging and it becomes more difficult to figure out exactly who is offering what services to which segment of the market. Needless to say, the Internet is also an excellent place for bankers to check out the competition's offerings and decide what strategies to pursue with their own customers.

*Mellon
bank site
map*

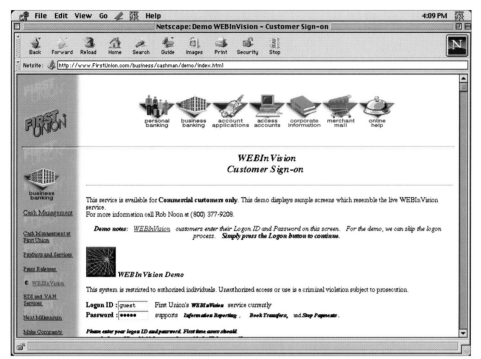

*First Union demo*

Commercial banks are a key source of many products and services for the treasury manager. At the most basic level they provide deposit accounts and checking services, as well as many options for investing funds in the short-term. Most larger banks also offer a wide array of cash management products and services designed to help the treasury manager with the collection, concentration and disbursement of funds. Additionally, these cash management banks may also provide electronic payment and collection services, as well as electronic com-

*PNC Bank financials*

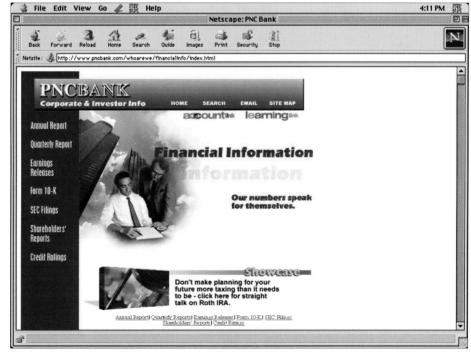

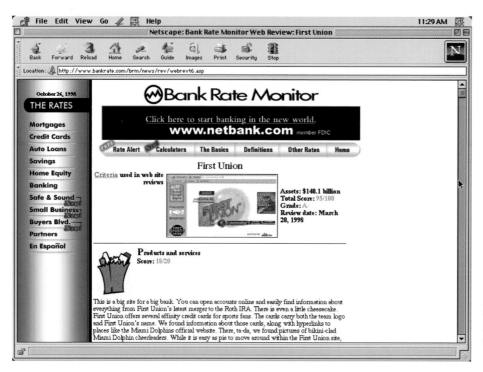

*Bank Rate Monitor website reviews*

merce (EC) or electronic data interchange (EDI) services.

Reviewing an individual bank's web site can give you additional insight into the bank's service offerings. Their product descriptions are similar to touring an exhibit area at an industry trade show. Many banks are moving toward offering both transactions and balance information on the Web for their corporate treasury customers.

Banks were among the first organizations to publish their own financial data such as an annual report on the Web.

## Bank Web Site Reviews

http://www.bankrate.com/brm/news/rev/revhome.asp

Bank Rate Monitor performs weekly reviews of U.S. financial institutions' web sites. The reviews address web site content, design and interactivity for home banking. Reviewing your bank's retail delivery system can give some

insight into developments for the corporate market.

## Standardized RFPs

http://www.bai.org/products/rfp/

Companies have been using standardized RFPs for cash management and other services for a number of years. In response to requests from banks and corporations, BAI and TMA have joined forces to develop standardized RFPs for seven cash management services:

ACH
Controlled Disbursement/Account
    Reconcilement/Positive Pay
Depository Services
Wholesale Lockbox
Wire Transfer
EDI
Information Reporting

Unfortunately no preview is available, only an order form. Cost is $75.00. Ken Parkinson and Ray Ruzek have published **How to Prepare** *an RFP for Bank Services* which can be ordered via e-mail at jochs@tisconsulting.com.

## Cash Management Pricing

http://www.phoenixhecht.com/analysis/BB98

This page contains the executive summary of the Phoenix-Hecht **Blue Book of Bank Prices.** This is an annual survey on the actual prices paid for the most commonly identified cash management services. Actual prices are gathered from corporate account analyses. The study is published each fall and is available for sale.

## Check Fraud

http://www.bankamerica.com/corporate/cash_management/fraud.html

This web page is a white paper from Bank of America describing how technology can be implemented to combat the problem of check fraud.

## Check Collection Same-Day Settlement Rule

http://www.cashmanagement.fcnbd.com/cash/new-rule.shtml

A discussion of the The Federal Reserve Board Same-Day Settlement Rule—effective January 3, 1994 from First Chicago.

## Check Imaging — Case Studies

http://www.iacorporation.com/casestudies.html

One of the most rapidly growing areas for applying image technology to check processing functions is in check-related corporate cash management services. This report from The Tower Group describes the market and technology factors behind the rapid adoption of imaging technology in this business area, and the different types of corporate cash management services that are currently being image-enabled by banks.

## A Primer on Electronic Payments

http://www.stls.frb.org/epaymnts/index.html

This page contains the St. Louis Federal Reserve Bank's primer on automated or electronic payments. The payments described here are handled electronically through the Automated Clearing House (ACH) system.

## Electronic Checks

http://www.nacha.org/ecc/ecc-wrkgps.htm

Listings of the Electronic Check Council Activities. Formed in 1995, the Council brings together industry stakeholders seeking solutions to the issues of rising costs and fraud associated with paper check processing systems. Each full member has a vote on issues and decisions related to the design and implementation of electronic check applications and may participate in any of the Council's current work groups such as Point of Deposit, Point of Sale, Marketing, Legal, Economic Framework, or Lockbox/Remittance Processing. Non-members may purchase reports.

## ACH Terms

http://www.sfe.org/glosbody.htm

Glossary of terms commonly used to describe Automated Clearing House transactions, work flows and functionality from the Southern Financial Exchange.

http://www.wiso.gwdg.de/ifbg/bank_2.html

Site maintained by the Institute of Finance and Banking at the University of Göttingen in Germany.

## CASH MANAGEMENT BANKS

| | |
|---|---|
| ABN AMRO/LaSalle National Bank | http://www.abnamro.com/ |
| AmSouth Bank | http://www.amsouth.com/ |
| BankBoston | http://www.bankboston.com/ |
| Bank of America | http://www.bankamerica.com/ |
| Bank of New York | http://www.bankofny.com/ |
| Bank One | http://www.bankone.com/ |
| Branch Bank and Trust | http://www.bbandt.com/index.html |
| Chase Bank of Texas | http://www.chase.com/tx/ |
| Chase Manhattan Bank, N.A. | http://www.chasemanhattan.com/ middlemarket/index.html |
| Citibank | http://www.citibank.com/ |
| Comerica | http://www.comerica.com/ |
| Commerce Bank of Kansas City | http://www.commercebank.com/ |
| Crestar | http://www.crestar.com/ |
| Fifth Third Bank | http://www.fifththird.com/ |
| First Chicago NBD | http://www.fcnbd.com/ |
| First National Bank of Maryland | http://www.firstmd.com/ |
| First of America Bank | http://www.foa.com/ |
| First Tennessee Bank | http://ftb.com/ |
| First Union National Bank | http://www.firstunion.com/ |
| Firstar Bank Milwaukee | http://www.firstar.com/ |
| Fleet Bank | http://www.fleet.com/ |
| Frost Bank | http://www.frostbank.com/ |
| Harris Trust & Savings Bank | http://www.harrisbank.com/ |
| Huntington National Bank | http://www.huntington.com/ |
| KeyCorp | http://www.key.com/ |
| Magna Bank | http://www.magnabank.com/home.html |

| | |
|---|---|
| Manufacturers & Traders Trust Company | http://www.mandtbank.com/ |
| Marine Midland Bank | http://www.marinemidland.com/ |
| Marshall & Ilsley Bank | http://www.mibank.com/ |
| Mellon Bank | http://www.mellon.com/ |
| Mercantile Bank | http://www.mercantile.com/kansas/ |
| National City Corporation | http://www.national-city.com/ |
| NationsBank | http://www.nationsbank.com/ |
| Northern Trust Company | http://www.northerntrust.com/ |
| Norwest | http://www.norwest.com/ |
| PNC Bank | http://www.pncbank.com/ |
| Provident Bank | http://www.provident-bank.com |
| Regions Bank | http://www.regionsbank.com/ |
| Star Bank | http://www.starbank.com/ |
| State Street Bank & Trust Company | http://www.statestreet.com/ |
| SunTrust | http://www.suntrust.com/ |
| UMB Banks | http://www.umb.com/ |
| Union Bank of California | http://uboc.com |
| U.S. Bank | http://www.usbank.com/ |
| Wachovia | http://www.wachovia.com/ |
| Wells Fargo | http://wellsfargo.com/home/ |
| BNP (France) | http://www.calvacom.fr/BNP/ |
| ANZ (Australia) | http://www.anz.com.au |
| Bradesco | http://www.bradesco.com.br/ |
| Credit Suisse | http://www.ska.com/ |
| Deutsche Bank | http://www.deutsche-bank.de/index_e.htm |
| Royal Bank of Canada | http://www.royalbank.com/ |
| Royal Bank of Scotland | http://www.royalbankscot.co.uk/home.htm |
| Toronto Dominion | http://www.tdbank.ca/tdbank/ |
| Union Bank of Switzerland | http://www.ubs.com |

## Electronic Federal Tax Payment System

http://www.fms.treas.gov/eftps/index.html

The Financial Management Service (FMS) of the Department of Treasury details their Electronic Federal Tax Payment System. EFTPS provides an electronic system for reporting and paying federal taxes. By replacing the current paper-based system, the EFTPS will benefit taxpayers and the federal government by providing greater reporting efficiencies and by expediting the availability of funds and investment decision-making information to the Treasury. E-mail notifications of updates to this page are available.

## Frequently Asked Questions

http://corp.nationsbank.com/treasury/html/treas_conn.html

NationsBank incorporates a treasury management forum on its web pages. Treasury Connection is a weekly digest of interactive questions about treasury management topics.

You can subscribe to the digest at no charge and have it e-mailed to you weekly as well as access previous issues.

## Lockbox Modeling

http://www.phoenixhecht.com/library/mode

Models have become an integral part of cash management. They are used to forecast cashflows, to plan investment strategies and to locate lockbox and disbursement sites. There are, however, many problems and frustrations in using models. Often one encounters the so called "prove it" problem. This white paper from Phoenix-Hecht explains the limitations in remittance modeling.

## Government Payments — Automated Clearing House (ACH)

http://www.fms.treas.gov/ach/index.html

The federal government is the largest single user of the Automated Clearing House (ACH)

*NationsBank treasury management forum*

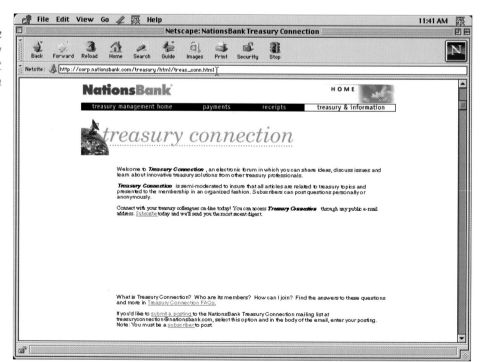

system, originating and receiving millions of transactions each month. This site provides processing specifications for the different electronic payment programs such as Vendor Express.

## Remittance Processing and Payment Processing Basics

http://www.creditron.com/basics.htm

This how-to article is provided by Creditron. Creditron is a technology company which specializes in check, remittance and payment processing solutions using PC driven systems and standard operating systems. Technologies utilized include Image Processing, Optical Character Recognition (OCR), and Magnetic Ink Character Recognition (MICR). They specifically tailor solutions for remittance processing sites which have lower volumes (<10,000 payments per day), or special requirements which cannot be addressed by high speed transports.

## Evaluating a Lockbox Bank

http://www.phoenixhecht.com/library/3M

*Measuring, Modeling and Monitoring Your Lockbox* is a 50-page guide published by Phoenix-Hecht. This guide is a must read for anyone connected with processing remittances.

## Money Laundering

http://www.treas.gov/fincen/

This site from the Financial Crimes Enforcement Center of the Treasury Department contains a number of articles for any organization dealing with large sums of cash.

# Payables and Receivables

## Managing Accounts Payables

http://www.ioma.com/newsletters/map/index.shtml

Each issue of this IOMA (Institute of Management and Administration) publication contains dozens of ideas on how to substantially improve the efficiency and accuracy of managing payables. Helpful assessments of the latest software and equipment, employee motivational material, seminars and business services are included. Visitors to this site can also search archives of past articles for topics of interest.

## Collection Agencies

http://207.77.90.67/wguide/wire/wire_144532_47244_0_5.html

This page is a listing on the Lycos Business site which contains links to collection agencies.

## Collections and Credit Risk

http://ccr.faulknergray.com/index.htm

A monthly magazine published by Faulkner & Gray devoted to the collections and credit risk arena, *Collections & Credit Risk* delivers reports and analyses on the cutting-edge operational, technological, market and legal trends and developments.

## Accounts Payable News and Tips

http://www.recapinc.com/index_right.html

*A/P News* is a free newsletter from A/P RECAP, a provider of financial operations consulting services. Their services include: payment recovery, escheatment reduction, vendor management, vendor leverage and A/P operations consulting services.

### Travel and Expense Management

http://www.captura.com/resource/
forum.htm

This site provides information on the management of employee payables and travel and entertainment expenses ideas and solutions from Captura Software.

### The Accountant's Ledger — An On-line Magazine for Accountants

http://www.accountantsledger.com/
index.html

This site allows the user to access current information of interest to the corporate accountant and/or controller. Pages on this site provide searches on back issues, as well as information on consulting services, electronic business, software, hardware, the Internet and more. The site is updated on a weekly basis.

## Cash and Treasury Management Publications

### Bank Statement

http://www.suntrust.com/bus/corp/
corp3.html

SunTrust's international treasury management newsletter, *Bank Statement*, is available for downloading in a PDF format.

### Business Finance (formerly Controller Magazine)

http://www.businessfinancemag.com.

*Controller Magazine* has changed its name to *Business Finance*. The new name and tag line—*Business Finance: Bottomline Solutions for Financial Executives*—is designed to more

accurately reflect the editorial mission of the publication.

### Cash Magazine

http://www.cashmanagement.fcnbd.com/
cash/index.shtml

*Cash Magazine* is an on-line publication of articles authored by First Chicago NBD cash management and trade specialists. These articles have been previously published in various treasury trade journals, as indicated within each article.

### Corporate EFT Report

http://www.ectoday.com/samples/
corp0416.htm

The site from Phillips Publishing contains sample articles from previous newsletters. Back issues are maintained in an archive, and information can be retrieved by key word and/or date range. The searchable archive is only available to registered customers. You can register for trial access.

### Financial Connection Newsletter

http://www.fms.treas.gov/finconn/
index.html

The *Financial Connection* is published by the Financial Management Service Department of the Treasury for federal agencies and others interested in advancing sound federal financial management. Subjects span asset, cash and debt management; financial accounting and reporting; reimbursable services to agencies; federal payments and legislative developments; and updates on electronic products and services developed by the Financial Management Service for its customer federal agencies.

### Treasury & Risk Management Magazine

http://www.cfonet.com

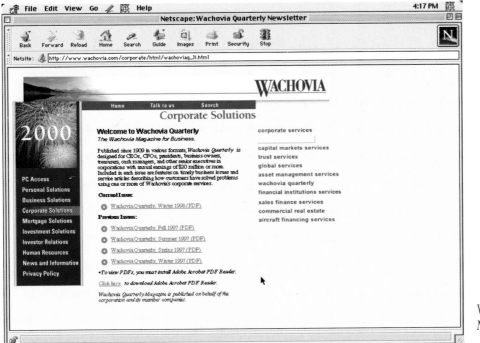

*Wachovia Magazine*

## Hot Topics — *BankAmerica*

http://www.bankamerica.com/corporate/
cash_management/topov.html

This page in Bank of America's web site provides the user with access to the bank's published articles list of hot topics in cash management, regulatory issues, international cash management and technology.

## Journal of Cash Management

http://www.tma-net.org/library/

Search for articles from 1991 through current issues of *TMA Journal* and its predecessor, *Journal of Cash Management*. Searches will produce abstracts of the articles.

## Treasury Matters

http://www.fpsc.com/firstunion/

*Treasury Matters* is a quarterly newsletter published by the cash management group at First Union. Organized by issue date.

## Wachovia Quarterly

http://www.wachovia.com/corporate/html/
wachoviaq_li.html

The *Wachovia Magazine for Business* has been published since 1909 in various formats. The publication is designed for CEOs, CFOs, presidents, business owners, treasurers, cash managers and other senior executives in corporations with annual revenues of $20 million or more. In each issue are features on timely business issues and service articles describing how customers have solved problems using one or more of Wachovia's corporate services.

## Treasury Consultants

http://phoenixhecht.com/consult

Many banks, accounting firms and individuals provide consulting services to the corporate treasury manager. While many have not invested in a web site to promote their capabilities, Phoenix-Hecht maintains a directory of contacts and addresses at this site.

# Treasury Management Software

The treasury area of an organization generally deals with two basic types of software. The first type of software is more cash management oriented and is usually referred to as "treasury management" or "treasury workstation" software. In most cases, this type of software is provided by specialized software companies (or in some cases by banks). Companies utilize these treasury workstations to manage their treasury operations and bank relationships. The software generally allows a company to access information (balances, check clearings, etc.) on their account, initiate payments (paper or electronic), manage their short-term debt and/or investments, or to access information on current rates or other data.

The second type of financial management software usually refers to the software used for financial reporting and control purposes. This software is generally part of an organization's overall management information system and may also be linked to applications such as accounts receivable or accounts payable.

## Selecting Financial Reporting Systems

http://www.asaenet.org/sections/
technology/helppr10.htm

In this article, the steps in the selection of a financial information system are outlined and described.

## Guide to Treasury Technology

☆ ☆ ☆

http://www.bobsguide.com/

Bob Browing's Guide to Treasury Technology contains fact sheets and contact information for hundreds of products, covering derivatives, money markets, capital markets

*Bob Browning's Guide to Treasury Technology*

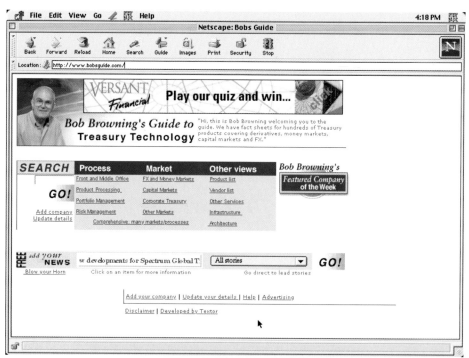

and FX. It is a cross-referenced set of fact sheets about technology products and services for the Treasury area. At present there are almost 600 products in varying degrees of detail including contact information.

## Software Search

http://software-guide.com/cdprod1/
sw.html

TurboGuide is a comprehensive, powerful and easy-to-use CD-ROM and commercial software directory. It is free to both end users and product developers. End users can use it as long as they wish, and product developers can list and promote their products.

## Financial Applications Oracle Applications Users Group (OAUG)

http://www.oaug.org/vendor/consultant/
fin.html

A guide to Oracle software vendors and consultants specializing in financial applications.

## PeopleSoft

http://www.peoplesoft.com/
products_and_services/peoplesoft7.5/
75businessprocess.htm

This page in the PeopleSoft site presents information on recent additions to the financial capabilities of their software in the areas of cash management, deal management and risk management.

## Selkirk Financial Technologies Inc.

http://www.selkirkfinancial.com/
index.html

Selkirk Financial Technologies Inc. is the creator of Treasury Manager™, an integrated Windows®-based treasury workstation. Treasury Manager's™ ten applications work together to manage cash, forecasting, electronic payments, deal capture and risk management activities.

## SunGard Treasury Systems

http://www.sungard.com/

The Company offers a comprehensive family of proprietary products for the financial services industry that automates complex accounting calculations, record keeping and reporting associated with investment operations.

## Treasury Workstation Providers (Non-Bank)

| | |
|---|---|
| ADS | http://www.ads-associates.com |
| Datalink | http://www.ibtcom.com |
| Gateway Systems | http://www.gatewaysystem.com |
| Selkirk | http://www.selkirkfinancial.com/index.html |
| SunGard | http://www.sungard.com |
| XRT | http://xrt.com |

**DAVID L. SHAFER**
**NATIONAL CASH MANAGEMENT CONSULTING PRACTICE**
**(816) 480-5504**

*THERE ISN'T A BUSINESS WE CAN'T IMPROVE®* **☰☰ ERNST & YOUNG**

CHAPTER 3

# Electronic Commerce

*ELECTRONIC COMMERCE is
applying electronic solutions
to current business transactions
or creating new ways to conduct
business. EC has become the
"holy grail" of the Internet
model for doing business with
consumers or other corporations.
The emerging, and many times
competing, technologies make
this a must watch area for
the treasury manager.* 🖥️

Electronic commerce (EC) is the use of electronic means to send data and/or payments from one organization or business entity to another. EC ranges from the use of unstructured electronic formats such as fax and e-mail to more elaborate formats such as Electronic Data Interchange (EDI). EC impacts all areas of an organization dealing with information exchanges to/from other organizations: marketing, production, transportation, purchasing and finance.

Banks also provide some EC services, especially where they involve the payment process. Electronic payments also change the cash flow timeline, and thus the level of current assets and working capital will be affected. When companies implement electronic payments, the typical cash management problems of collections, disbursements and concentration change considerably. Finally, EC also impacts the legal, audit and control areas of the company. Much of the legal infrastructure related to business and payments is oriented towards paper-based systems as are the areas of financial audit and control. EC has significant impacts on these areas and must be considered.

## EDI Glossary

http://www.stercomm.com/basics/glossary.htm

A glossary of electronic commerce terms from Sterling Software.

## Electronic Commerce Industry Calendar

http://www.ecresources.com/tools/calendar/calendar.html

This calendar is a comprehensive list of upcoming industry events, workshops, seminars, conferences, trade shows and meetings maintained by Thomson EC Resources, a subsidiary of Thomson Financial Publishing. Interestingly, this site has no links in its listings.

## A Primer on EDI

http://www.cf.ac.uk/uwcc/masts/ecic/eleccomm.html

The Electronic Commerce Innovation Centre, funded by British Telecommunications plc and managed by Professor Tony Davies, has played an active role in developing and promoting EDI standards for international and domestic trade in close collaboration with the Electronic Commerce Association (UK), the European Board for EDIFACT Standards and the UN/ECE Working Party for International Trade Facilitation.

## EDI Capable Organizations

http://www.ecresources.com/services/welcomescr.html

The Thomson EDI Partners Database is a comprehensive database of profiles and contact information about the EC capabilities of companies. Your company can be listed at no charge. Annual subscriptions begin at $695.

## Guide to Electronic Commerce

http://ecommerce.miningco.com/

This site attempts to cut through the confusion and complexity of the issues surrounding electronic commerce and concentrates on the practical issues of putting electronic commerce into action. They take an informal, fun, but above all focused, view of the subject. After all, the bottom line of all commerce is to make money.

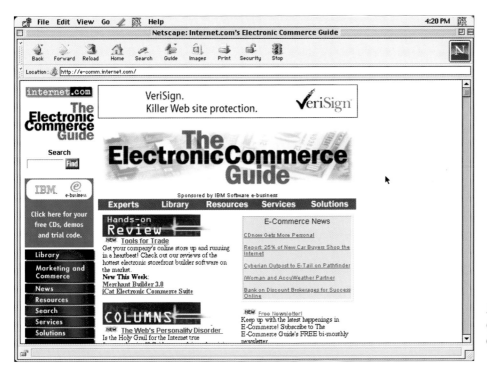

*Electronic Commerce Guide*

## Electronic Commerce Today

http://www.ectoday.com/ecisite.htm

This site is designed for executives involved with such technologies as: imaging, Electronic Data Interchange (EDI), e-mail, integrated messaging, Internet, external networks (VANs), groupware, electronic funds transfer, electronic benefits transfer and forms processing. EC Today is a subscription site updated on a daily basis. Trial subscriptions are available.

## Electronic Commerce World

http://www.ecresources.com/information/ecw/bib.html

*EC World* is a monthly magazine of electronic commerce with comprehensive editorial and advertising content on topics including electronic commerce implementation, financial EDI, electronic messaging, workflow automation and imaging. Only an index to past articles organized by year is available on this site.

## Electronic Commerce Guide

http://e-comm.internet.com/

Sponsored by IBM software, the Guide's library of books, articles, journals, newsletters and white papers covers topics relevant to conducting electronic commerce.

## Purchasing Card

http://www.udel.edu/purch/card/faster/defined.html

This University of Delaware site contains instructions and procedures for employee use of their purchasing card. It provides a good example of documentation and procedures.

## Journal of Internet Banking and Commerce

http://www.arraydev.com/commerce/JIBC/

JIBC has begun to post evaluations of service quality of world financial institutions that conduct transactional delivery of banking services through the Internet.

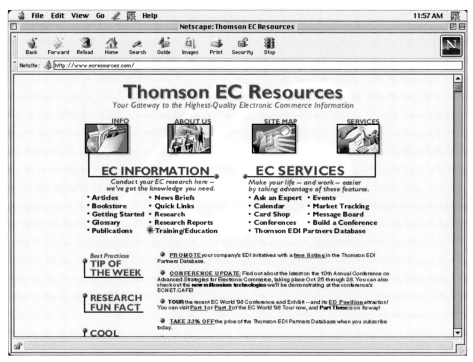

## The Journal of Electronic Commerce

http://www.ecresources.com/information/
jec/jec.html

This site only contains Executive Summaries from the current issue and an index to previous issues.

## Electronic Solutions Article

http://wellsfargo.com/com/electronic/
articles/

This Wells Fargo Bank site contains a listing of useful articles in the area of electronic solutions and electronic payments.

## Financial EDI over the Internet

http://www.bankamerica.com/batoday/
edi_briefing.html

An article from Bank of America describing a pilot program between them and the Lawrence Livermore National Laboratory to test whether the Internet can be used to transmit secure and reliable electronic messages and payments between trading partners and their banks.

## EDI-Electronic Data Interchange

http://grace.wharton.upenn.edu/~opim314/
projects/EDI.htm

This site contains listings of EDI vendors and related EDI Internet sites as well as a general discussion of EDI.

## On-line Transaction Banking Issues

http://www.netscapeworld.com/
nw-08-1997/nw-08-banking.html

This article attempts to help new Web-based businesses understand banking and financial fundamentals behind credit card transactions. Understanding the banking issues may help guide your hardware and software choices, as well as your overall budget. Includes a glossary of credit card processing terms.

## Electronic Bill Payment

http://gartner12.gartnerweb.com/
public/static/home/home.html

Gartner Group is one of the primary research organizations in the area of electronic commerce. Gartner Group Interactive is a very extensive collection of IT research and analysis available on-line. Full access to the site requires being a subscriber.

## Electronic Commerce Research Abstracts

http://www.towergroup.com/pages/
new2.htm

The Tower Group provides advisory services and consulting concerning the applications technology found in the global financial services industry. If you join the Tower Group electronic mailing list you will be notified when new research information is published on their web site.

## Electronic Billing White Papers

http://www.billing.com/Es/white1.htm

A collection of white papers from International Billing Services explaining electronic billing. Their main site (http://www.billing.com) has a demo of how electronic billing will work by walking you through the process and showing a sampling of how bills of the future may be designed.

## Federal Government Electronic Commerce

http://www.gwegroup.com/acquis.htm

An explanation and instructions to register for all contractors that want to do business with any federal government agency. The primary purpose is to avoid repetitive registrations with each procurement office and to create an accurate business profile for each business. Registration involves preparing and sending a complete Trading Partner Profile. The secondary purpose is to streamline the acquisition and payment process by collecting standard procurement information.

## Wharton Corporate Forum on Electronic Commerce

http://www.wharton.upenn.edu/news/
news_rel/eleccom.html

In an effort to help companies utilize the potential of emerging technologies such as the Internet, The Wharton School of the University of Pennsylvania created the Wharton Forum on Electronic Commerce in November of 1996. The Forum brings together non-competing companies to tap Wharton's virtual test market and usability lab on the World Wide Web, shape a research agenda and gain access to current developments in the emerging electronic commerce market. Forum members meet twice a year to discuss current issues. Founding members include AT&T Universal Card, Fannie Mae, Johnson & Johnson, Rosenbluth Travel, Safeguard Scientifics and State Farm Insurance Company.

## The Electronic Check Council of NACHA

http://www.nacha.org/ecc/default.htm

The Electronic Check Council provides a cooperative forum for building a framework for the conversion of checks to electronic payments. It serves as a voice of stakeholders for the resolution of electronic check product and operations issues and those of risk, liability and regulation.

## Center for Electronic Commerce

http://www.erim.org/cec

The Center for Electronic Commerce sponsored by ERIM specializes in helping supply chains develop best practice guidelines for EC technology adoption. Links are provided for a selected number of papers in Adobe PDF. Others, if they are available, may be ordered.

## Data Interchange Standards Association

http://www.disa.org/

This is the home page of the Data Interchange Standards Association (DISA). DISA is a not-for-profit organization that supports the development and use of EDI standards in electronic commerce. DISA's primary services are providing operational support for the X12 and UN/EDIFACT standards development process; maintaining and publishing EDI standards; and providing educational seminars, conferences and related information services. DISA members include Fortune 500 companies, government agencies and organizations of all sizes.

## Financial Services Technology Consortium

http://www.fstc.org/

The Financial Services Technology Consortium (FSTC) is a not-for-profit organization whose goal is to enhance the competitiveness of the United States financial services industry. Members of the consortium include banks, financial services providers, research laboratories, universities, technology companies and government agencies. FSTC sponsors project-oriented collaborative research and development on inter-bank technical projects affecting the entire financial services industry. Particular emphasis is placed on payment systems and services, and leveraging new technologies that help banks cement customer relationships, boost operational efficiency and expand their market reach.

## Electronic Commerce Links

http://www.ecresources.com/tools/linkpg1.html

This is an index site providing extensive links to Electronic Commerce sites maintained by Thomson EC Resources.

1863 Civil War token minted anonymously
to help remedy government coin shortage.

**WE HAVE A VERY SIMPLE CASH MANAGEMENT PHILOSOPHY: WE WORK HARD SO YOU DON'T HAVE TO.**

It takes a lot of hard work for your Cash Management operation to perform at its full potential. The problem is, while few seem to notice when things go smoothly, everyone notices when things go wrong. That's why First Union's dedicated cash management team works hard to get to know you, your business and your financial needs. That way, we can anticipate problems before they appear. And tailor the solutions your specific business requires. • And since time is of the essence, our Customer Service Analysts are just a phone call away to answer your questions quickly and easily. To find out even more about our cash management philosophy, call 1-800-377-9208 or visit our Web site at www.firstunion.com

FIRST UNION®

# CHAPTER 4

# Corporate Finance

*CORPORATE FINANCE is an area of treasury management where financial theory and practical applications merge in the process of allocating financial resources. There are a number of magazines and newsletters dealing with corporate finance that are accessible on the Web. Treasurers will also find dozens of investment bank sites.* 💻

Corporate financial management generally refers to the management of longer-term financial assets of a company. The treasurer is often the primary contact between the corporation and the capital markets, which makes this a critical part of treasury management. Managing capital market relations includes: debt and equity capital markets; hybrid, synthetic and derivative securities markets; initial public offerings; the investment banking process; regulatory and due diligence issues; responsibilities of the board of directors; and bankruptcy.

Corporate financial management also covers the impact of capital structure and dividend policies on the value of the company, as well as the impact on both debt and stock holders.

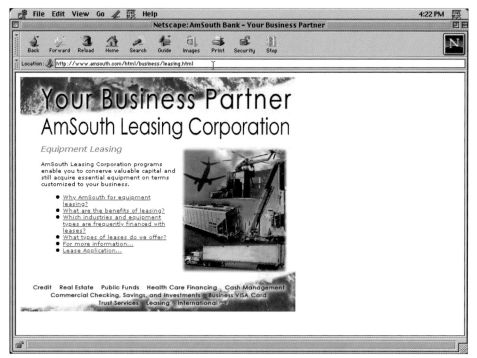

*AmSouth Business site*

A merger, acquisition, or divestiture is a critical time in the life of a firm, and the treasurer is usually involved in the process. An important task in the corporate financial management area is the review, analysis and interpretation of financial statements and reports. This is useful for measuring the performance of one company against another, or to see if financial managers are meeting the company's ongoing goals. Related to financial analysis is the preparation of pro-forma financial statements for planning and control purposes, as well as for forecasting the future of the company. Finally, the areas of capital budgeting and leasing are also considered as part of the corporate financial management responsibilities.

## Glossary of Financial Terms

http://www.finmin.lt/gloss/glosindx.htm

This extensive glossary of financial terms is maintained on a web site sponsored by The Ministry of Finance of The Republic of Lithuania.

## Virtual Finance Library

http://www.cob.ohio-state.edu/~fin/overview.htm

The Virtual Library is from Ohio State's Department of Finance. The information contained on these pages is provided for free. The information and links are well categorized.

## CFO and Treasury & Risk Management Magazine

http://www.cfonet.com/index.html

This site provides access to both **CFO** and **Treasury & Risk Management** magazines. You can access the archives and search past articles for specific topics and also check out a wide

range of resources of interest to treasury managers. The site also has information on **CFO**-sponsored conferences and on-line discussions on treasury topics.

## Financial Times

http://www.usa.ft.com

**The Financial Times** is a leading international English language business newspaper which aims to provide readers with the best source of global business information, analysis and comment. Content is free but first time users are required to register.

## CorpFiNet — Corporate Finance Network

http://www.corpfinet.com/

CorpFiNet is written for an audience of executives and decision makers in the financial services industry (banks, insurance companies, investment banks and related firms) who are using the Internet and related technologies to

*Corporate Finance Networks*

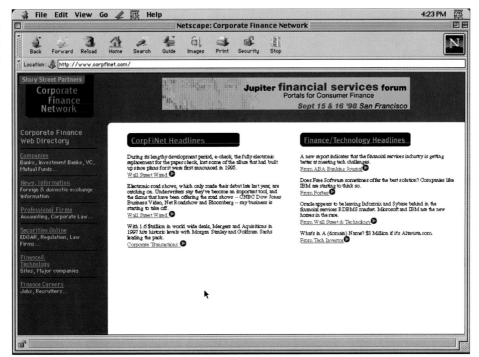

acquire and use information in new and better ways. CorpFiNet also focuses on CFOs, corporate treasurers, investment bankers, accountants, corporate attorneys and others who are involved in the world of corporate finance.

## A Treasurer's Guide to the Asset-Backed Security Market

http://www.worldserver.pipex.com/ hemscott/tmi/topics/nwm/nwm1.htm

This guide for first time issuers to the asset-backed security market is published by Nat-West Markets in the U.K.

## Journal of Finance

http://www.cob.ohio-state.edu/dept/fin/ journal/jof.htm

The **Journal of Finance** is the journal of the American Finance Association. Contents of future issues are available as well as materials related to past issues. These materials include data sets, unpublished appendices and tables,

as well as updates of past articles provided by the authors.

## Business Management

http://www.ioma.com/index.html

The main site of The Institute of Management and Administration (IOMA) offers a wide range of information and services to business managers. Under the Business Directory page http://www.ioma.com/industry/corp_fin_mgmt/ index.shtml there are links provided for corporate financial management. Visitors to the site can also search archives of IOMA publications for topics of interest.

## Journal of Applied Corporate Finance

http://www.sternstewart.com/publications/ jacf_index.html

Published since 1988, this highly regarded quarterly translates the best of current academic research into a form that is accessible and use-

*KPMG's virtual library archive*

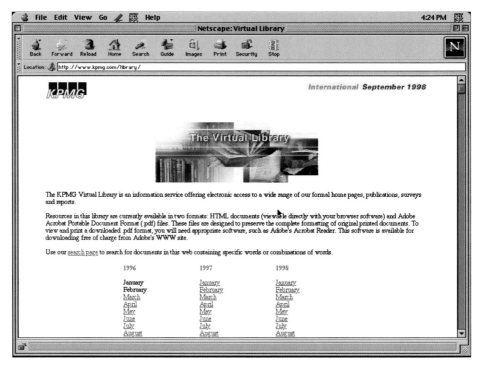

ful to senior corporate executives. Published in conjunction with BankAmerica, the Journal covers a range of topics, including financial innovations, restructuring, core competencies and global competition, corporate governance and relationship investing, and capital management. The site provides an index of articles and an order form.

## Searchable Archive

http://www.kpmg.com/library/

Resources of the KPGM library are currently available in two formats: HTML documents (viewable directly on your browser) and Adobe Acrobat Portable Document Format (PDF) files. PDF files are designed to preserve the complete formatting of original printed material.

## Financial Technology

http://www.financetech.com/password/ar_srch.htm

An archive of articles previously published in *Financial Technology* magazine.

## FINWeb

http://www.finweb.com/

FINWeb is a financial economics web site managed by James R. Garven, Ph.D. The primary objective of FINWeb is to list Internet resources providing substantive information concerning economics and finance-related topics.

## Newsletters

http://www.cmsinfo.com/a-Investment_and_Finance.html

This is the CMS internet catalogue of finance industry newsletters, management reports and market surveys. Listed on this site are titles from leading publishers specializing in finance, financial markets, risk, treasury and related areas with subscription information. There is a search facility.

## Financial Services News

http://financeservices.tqn.com/msubrisk.htm

This site provides financial services industry related news organized by the Mining Co. Each of the over 500 Mining Co. GuideSites™ is devoted to a single topic—complete with site reviews, feature articles and discussion areas.

## Public Companies with Financials Listed on the Web

http://www.natcorp.com/

The web is an excellent vehicle to distribute a company's financials to investors and other interested parties.

## Investment Bank Index

http://www.cob.ohio-state.edu/~fin/cern/invbank.htm

## Index to Finance Sites

http://www.gwdg.de/~ifbg/ufin.html

# Investment Banks

There are dozens of investment bank sites on the Web. Most offer brief descriptions of their services and information about the investment bank. A few offer research reports and economic forecasts, but usually only for registered clients. It's a good idea to review each of your current providers to see how they present themselves. Note: The current consolidation craze sweeping the financial services industry may make some of the URLs outdated.

| Site Name | Web Research Address |
| --- | --- |
| BT Alex Brown | http://www.btabresearch.com |
| Bank of Montreal | http://www.bmo.com/bmocc/top_home.htm |
| Brown, Brothers Harriman & Co. | http://www.bbh.com |
| CIBC Wood Gundy | http://www.cibc.com |
| CS First Boston | http://www.csfb.com/ |
| First Chicago Capital Markets | http://www.fccm.com/ |
| First Union | http://www.firstunion.com/library/profile/capmktslocations.html |
| Gruntal & Co. | http://www.gruntal.com/research/research.html |
| Goldman Sachs | http://www.gs.com/gsci/ |
| Hambrecht & Quist | http://www.hamquist.com/research/index.html |
| ING International | http://www.ingbank.com |
| Merrill Lynch | http://www.ml.com/ |
| Morgan Stanley | http://www.ms.com/ |
| Montgomery Securities | http://www.montegomerty.com |
| JP Morgan | http://www.jpmorgan.com |
| Nikko Securities | http://www.nikko.co.jp |
| PaineWebber | http://painewebber.com |
| Piper Jaffray | http://www.piperjaffray.com/ |
| Prudential Investments | http://www.prusec.com/ |
| Robertson Stephens | http://www.rsco.com |
| Royal Bank of Canada | http://www.royalbank.com/ |
| Salomon Brothers | http://www.salomon.com/ |
| Toronto Dominion | http://www.tdbank.ca/tdbank/ |
| Wertheim Schroder | http://www.hydra.com/wertheim/info.html |

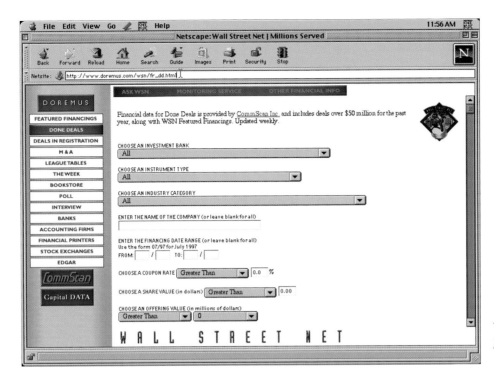

Wall Street Financings

## Wall Street Net ☆☆

http://www.doremus.com/wsn/fr_dd.html

This site from Doremus Financial Printing features a searchable database of information contained in registration statements filed with the Securities and Exchange Commission. Archival information contained in Wall Street Net is provided by CommScan.

## The Treasury Management Pages ☆☆☆

http://www.mcs.com/~tryhardz/tmpaa.html

The Treasury Management Pages were developed as an information management resource specifically to assist treasury managers and other finance professionals worldwide in dealing effectively with the massive quantities of business information available through the Internet. Their primary objective is to provide visitors with rapid and reliable access to their site and through the site pages, access to the very best professional information resources on the World Wide Web.

## Corporate Finance Links

http://207.77.90.67/wguide/wire/wire_144532_47256_3_1.html

This page is a listing on the Lycos Business site which contains links to corporate finance sites.

## Futures Magazine

http://www.futuresmag.com/

*Futures Magazine* is a resource for users and traders of options and futures contracts. The site maintains a complete reference guide to futures and options firms, exchanges, contracts, industry organizations, regulatory agencies. Listings include company names, addresses, phone numbers, e-mail and web site address and key personnel.

L O W – T E C H. *Okay for your kid's cash management.*
Not okay for your company's cash management. How much
technology do you need to manage your company's money? Depends on how well you want the
money to perform. At LaSalle National Bank we offer you the most sophisticated electronic cash
management products available. CashPro+® lets you perform everything from wire transfers to stop
payments instantly. CashPro Image™ transmits check images directly to your office. And our powerful
CashPro Trader+™ lets you initiate international wire and draft payments anytime, buy and sell foreign
currency with real-time rates, and track all of your international
transactions. It's not enough to have cash management products that
work. You need the cash management products that work the hardest.

**Member of the ABN AMRO Group**

**For a free CashPro+ demonstration, visit www.lasallebanks.com/cashmanagement** ©1998

## CHAPTER 5

# International Treasury Management

*THE GLOBALIZATION of the U.S. economy has caused even mid-sized companies to be engaged in some foreign trade transactions. In response to the many needs of these companies, many banks have combined their international products offerings with their domestic cash management organizations. On the Web, the treasury manager will find information on foreign exchange and international markets.*

For companies directly involved in the international arena, either with foreign operations or subsidiaries, international treasury management can be a challenging process. Even companies with primarily domestic operations may have significant foreign revenues or expenses as part of their day-to-day business.

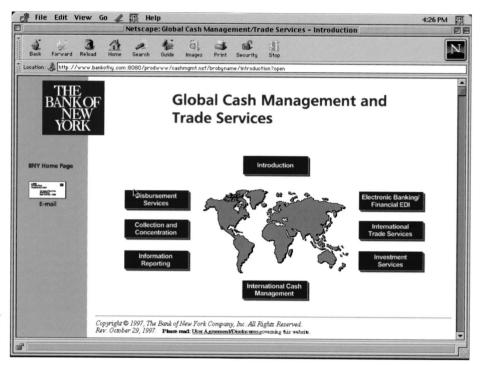

*Bank of New York*

Having to deal with multiple currencies, governments, regulations, time zones and long distances make the international treasury area a difficult one to manage. Historically, multinational banks have provided a wide range of services to the international treasurer, from foreign exchange services to letters of credit to netting services. In addition, as worldwide financial markets continue to integrate, more and more companies are finding their sources of both short and long-term capital are coming from outside their domestic markets.

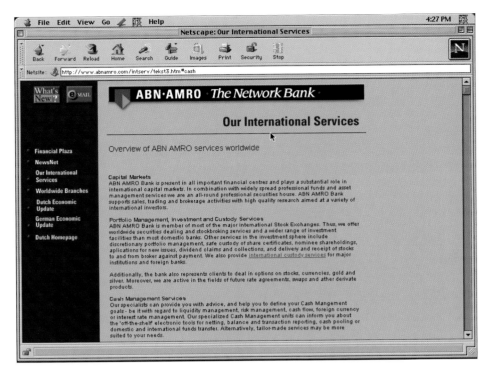

*ABN-AMRO*

## FX Glossary ⭐

http://www.fxfxnet.com/members/
glossary.htm

Courtesy of FXFXNET, Ltd. See below.

## Simple Currency Conversions

http://www.xe.net./currency/

The Universal Currency Converter™ allows you to perform interactive foreign exchange rate conversions. Simply type the amount of source currency in the input box and select the currency you wish to receive.

## A Treasurer's Guide To International Cash Management

http://www.worldserver.pipex.com/
hemscott/tmi/topics/abn/abn.htm

This guide discusses the use of netting for multinational companies. It is published by ABN AMRO Bank.

## International Treasurer

http://www.intltreasurer.com/

This is the site of the **International Treasurer, The Journal of Global Treasury** and **Financial Risk Management**. Members can access information from past articles and can participate in a roundtable forum for treasury professionals.

## FX Regulations & Laws

http://www.fxfxnet.com/members/
regulati.htm

This site contains various reports on payment and operational risks as well as International Securities Dealers Association contracts, used principally for bonds and financial instruments. The site also includes the International Currency Options Market terms and conditions and associated comments and guidance notes.

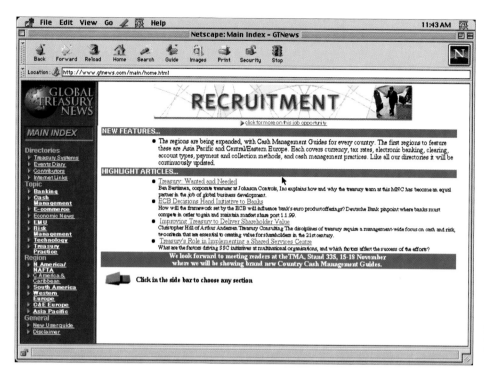

*Global Treasury News*

## Global Treasury News ☆☆

http://www.gtnews.com/

**Global Treasury News** is a unique source of industry information for corporate treasurers on the Internet. It is an independent UK-based publication which caters to treasury professionals by providing informed commentary and analysis from key players throughout the industry.

*GTNews* draws together ideas on a range of crucial issues. It contains an extensive archive of articles, organized by subject and region. It does require registration, but there is currently no charge. Once the user is registered, they can just click through to the main index and pick an area of interest from the side bar.

## FX Treasury Management

http://www.fxfxnet.com/members/treasury.htm

An overview of the rules which determine the value dates for various transaction types and examples of the calculations.

## Financial Technology International

http://www.financetech.com/fti.htm

This site provides information on financial technology products, services and educational conferences. Good portions of the site are free. The newsletter requires a subscription.

## FXFXNET, Ltd.

http://www.fxfxnet.com/

Provides specific foreign exchange information to global FX traders and corporate treasurers. It is developing a sophisticated web site for members. Though the site is still listed as a beta-prototype, it is currently accessible and some of the features include: a directory page listing global banks dealing in treasury with links to key personnel within the bank, including addresses and phone numbers, plus intra-day bank rates for leading currencies.

## International Treasury Direct

http://www.worldserver.pipex.com/hemscott/tmi/tmiindex.htm

International Treasury Direct is the international forum for corporate treasury professionals. This site provides access to articles, information, market news, conferences and treasury association details, plus Treasury Management International's (TMI) Cumulative Index of articles, authors, companies and topics since 1992.

## International Treasurer
*The Journal of Global Treasury and Financial Risk Management*

http://www.intltreasurer.com

Send an e-mail with "send issue" in the subject line and they will send you a sample issue as an attached Adobe Acrobat™ PDF file.

## Cross-Border Council

http://www.nacha.org/xborder/default.htm

The Cross-Border Council was established in 1993 to create the framework for the efficient exchange of cross-border, batch-oriented electronic corporate and consumer payment transactions (ACH/EFT payments). The goal of the Council is to develop a set of principles, rules and standards to which participants agree in order to effect cross-border electronic payments. Cross-border payment between the United States and Canada utilizing the Cross-Border Payment Operating Rules began in 1996. Corporations are permitted to be members.

## Getting The Most From Your Netting System — A Treasurer's Guide to International Cash Management

http://www.worldserver.pipex.com/hemscott/tmi/topics/abn/abn.htm

A publication from ABN-AMRO.

## International Treasury Management Association

http://www.intltreasury.org/

This is the home page of the International Group of Treasury Associations which was formed to utilize synergy and enhance the activities of the treasury associations across nations.

## Global Investor Bookshop

http://www.global-investor.com/bookshop/index.htm

This site allows the user to search over 1,000 book offerings of interest to financial managers and investors in a global environment.

## The Economist Intelligence Unit

http://www.eiu.com/1s4b6zgx/

The EIU is an information provider for companies establishing and managing operations across national borders anywhere in the world. Established 50 years ago in London, they now have a worldwide network of offices in London, New York, Hong Kong, Vienna, Singapore and Tokyo. The EIU produces objective and timely analyses and forecasts of the political, economic and business environments in more than 180 countries. They also produce reports on certain strategic industries and on the latest management thinking.

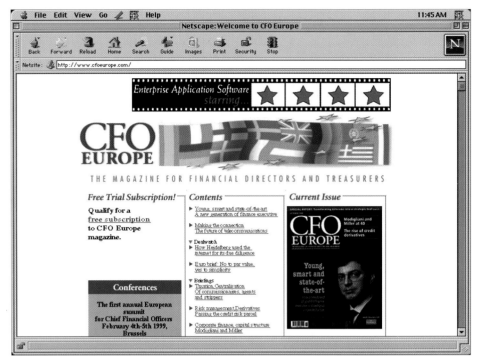

*CFO Europe*

## The Economist Group

http://www.economist.com/

The Economist Group is an authoritative source of information and opinion on international business and politics. Many of the group's units and specialist publications have web sites:

*Business Central Europe*
*CFO* (Chief Financial Officer)
*CFO Europe*
*The Economist Conferences*
*Economist Intelligence Unit* (EIU)
*The EIU Viewswire*
*European Voice*
*Information Strategy*
*The Journal of Commerce* (JOC)
*Public Network Europe*
*Roll Call*
*The World in 1998*
*Traffic World*
*Treasury & Risk Management*

# Now, SunTrust can turn a Lockbox into a Look Box.

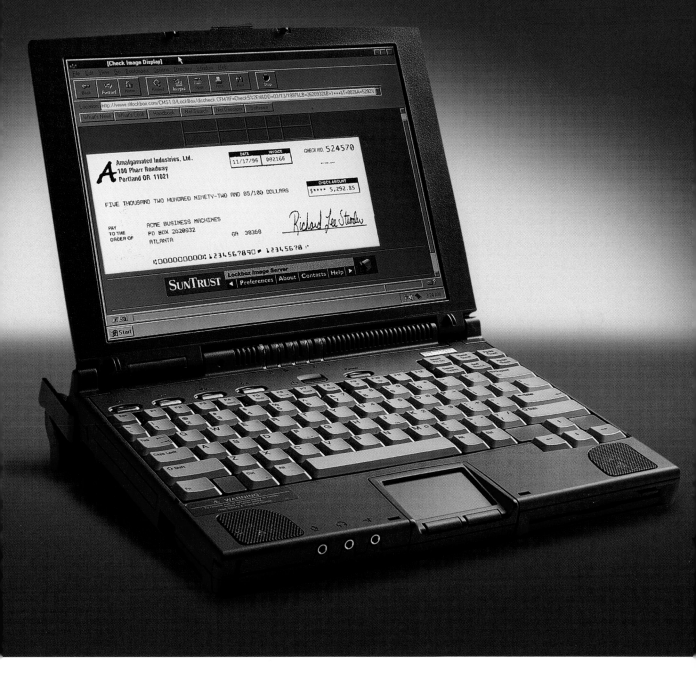

Our *Lockbox Image Browser*[SM] *lets you view checks instantly. Through a private network, and using Windows-compatible software, our Lockbox Image Browser lets you see your checks minutes after they've been processed. So you can make timelier credit decisions, provide your customers with better service and improve productivity. The Lockbox Image Browser is one of many innovative lockbox services from SunTrust designed to ease your way into the world of electronic commerce. For more information, call Ward Gailey at 1-800-811-6467.*

*Credit Services • Investment Banking • Treasury Management • International Services*

**SUNTRUST**

# No two treasury management problems are exactly alike. Luckily, our solutions aren't either.

Every business has a unique set of treasury management problems.

To meet them, you need a financial services company that identifies trouble spots. Then finds the specific answers that solve them.

In short, you need PNC Bank.

Unlike other banks that talk about custom solutions, then give you stock answers, delivering tailored solutions is one of our driving principles.

For example, we offer 50 different process options through ACIS to help our clients select their own ACH solutions. While PINACLE® For Windows® allows clients almost infinite flexibility in accessing information and creating customized reports.

To learn more about how PNC Bank can help handle your company's treasury management needs, call 1-800-685-4039. Or talk to your treasury management officer today. Because we guarantee the way we do business will leave a lasting impression on you.

## PNCBANK®
*Where Performance Counts*

## CHAPTER 6

# Institutional Investment

*MANY OF THE SOURCES for individual investor information also provide information for the institutional investor. This chapter has many interesting sites which provide a large portion of material at no charge to the individual user.*

## Glossary of Investment Terms — Prudential Securities ☆

http://www.prusec.com/glos_txt.htm

This site provides a glossary of investment and investing terms.

## Institutional Investing — A Newsletter from IOMA, The Institute of Management and Administration

http://www.ioma.com/industry/inst_invest/index.shtml

A newsletter from IOMA, The Institute of Management and Administration. IOMA newsletter sites have searchable archives.

## Defined Contribution Plan Investing — A Newsletter from IOMA, The Institute of Management and Administration

http://www.ioma.com/newsletters/dcpi/index.shtml

The Institute of Management and Administration is a source of information on the DC marketplace for service providers and plan sponsors. *DCPI* provides its newsletter readers with the data and analysis they need on sponsor and vendor news, asset allocation trends, investment manager performance, GIC yields and DC plan company stock holdings.

## Financial Data — Bloomberg Financial Markets ☆ ☆

http://www.bloomberg.com/welcome.html

Bloomberg has established a unique position within the financial services industry by consolidating a broad range of features in a single package. Bloomberg offers news and analyses on domestic and world markets. Users can also find bond yields, stock quotes and futures contracts on-line. Bloomberg also produces related media products for distribution in the United States, Canada, Europe, the Middle East, Latin America, Australia and Asia.

## Ratings — Fitch IBCA, Inc.

http://www.fitchibca.com/home/frame.html

Fitch IBCA is an international rating agency with analysts and staff in 21 offices. They have established coverage of over 1,000 banks and financial institutions, approximately 400 corporates around the world, and 50 sovereigns. The site has a search feature for ratings, research, surveillance or press releases based on specific text.

## Moody's

http://www.moodys.com

Moody's Company Data Direct offers Internet access to U.S. public company information on more than 10,000 companies via the Moody's FIS on-line web site. There is a free tour for registered users.

## MoneyLine

http://www.moneyline.com/

MoneyLine is the virtual financial network for the on-line financial community. Hundreds of organized pages and thousands of data items are gathered from leading financial companies, such as GovPX, InterCapital, Garban, S&P, Comstock and AFX News. Broad market coverage includes the fixed income, money, futures, derivatives, equities and foreign exchange markets. Benchmarking, real-time prices and

*Dow Jones*
*Telerate*

analyses from key market makers provide accurate coverage of over-the-counter and exchange traded markets.

## Market Briefings

http://www.briefing.com/

Charter Media provides market commentary. Their staff focuses readers on the important news affecting the markets and provides insight on the possible implications for trading. Briefing.com covers upgrades, earnings reports, economic releases, technical trading points, market sectors, technology stocks and much more, all from an analytical standpoint. Current market data and concise analyses are offered. Stock, bond and dollar tickers complement all the economic data and forecasts.

## Daily Economic Indicators
### Dow Jones Telerate

http://www.telerate.com/

## Managed Fund Ratings

http://www.ratings.standardpoor.com/funds/

Standard & Poor's Managed Funds Ratings Group rates money market funds, bond funds, local government investment pools and unit investment.

## Financial Data —
## IBC Financial Data, Inc.

http://www.ibcdata.com/

IBC Financial Data is an information provider to individual and institutional investors. The company has a strong tradition of providing consumers, institutions, corporations and regulators with independent analyses of trends in the financial services and investing industries, with particular concentration on money market mutual funds. It publishes a wide range of business-to-business print publications, also available electronically via e-mail and the World Wide Web.

## Morningstar

http://www.morningstar.net/

Morningstar is a provider of mutual fund, stock and variable-insurance investment information. An independent company, Morningstar does not own, operate, or hold any interest in mutual funds, stocks, or insurance products and can provide unbiased data and analysis, and candid editorial commentary. This site has free access to tools and comprehensive research.

## Commodities
### Mid America Commodities Exchange Charts and Data

http://midam.com/ecb/mdmpag.htm

The Exchange provides ten-minute delayed quotes for all MidAm contracts.

## StockMaster

http://www.stockmaster.com/

This site offers a quick way to access stock and mutual fund quotes and historical charts going back to 1993.

## Municipal Bond Market Data

http://www.kennydrake.com/

J.J. Kenny Drake, a large inter-dealer of municipal bonds, which has a comprehensive source of real-time in-depth regional and national coverage of municipal market data. Fee required.

## InvestorLinks

http://www.investorlinks.com/

This index site contains links to many sites of interest to financial managers and investors. New sites are added every day, and are checked on an continuous basis to make sure the links listed are fresh. Both site visitors and other site providers can request links be added to the page. In addition, free real-time quotes are available on every main page.

## Real-Time Stock Quotes — PC Quote On-line

http://www.pcquote.com/

This site provides free quotes on a time-delayed basis for publicly traded securities, as well as other financial services for a nominal monthly fee. PC Quote gathers data on more than 250,000 issues on all U.S. and Canadian equities and options. They also offer a wide range of other services for both investors and businesses.

## Hoover's On-line

http://www.hoovers.com/

A great source to provide you with core financial and operating information on important public and private U.S. and foreign companies. Users can access information to screen stocks, sort results, research companies, check quotes and view charts.

## Small-Cap Public Companies

http://www.stocknet-usa.com/findex.phtml

At this one-stop source for information on small to medium-sized publicly traded companies, a user can find brief summaries of companies including corporate profiles, financial highlights, officers, addresses and stock history.

# Other Investment Information

## Securities and Exchange Commission (SEC)

http://www.sec.gov/

This searchable database of SEC quarterly, annual and other reports on all publicly traded companies can provide invaluable investing insights. Mutual fund filings are also provided.

## NYSE — New York Stock Exchange

http://www.nyse.com/

Through its web site, the NYSE strives to enhance public understanding of the capital formation and allocation process.

## NASDAQ — The National Association of Securities Dealers

http://www.nasdaq.com/

Like many of the exchange sites, NASDAQ maintains market indices, a stock ticker and other market information.

## AMEX — American Stock Exchange

http://www.amex.com/

This site is the home page of the American Stock Exchange. In 1995, the AMEX became the first U.S. stock market to maintain a presence on the World Wide Web, offering a site rich with comprehensive data on listed companies, options, derivatives and capital markets products. WebLink, the exclusive, automated service for their listed companies, offers potential investors and shareholders a range of information on every AMEX stock.

## Commodity Futures Trading Commission

http://www.cftc.gov/cftc/

This site is provided by the federal agency regulating futures trading. There is a large selection of reports and publications available.

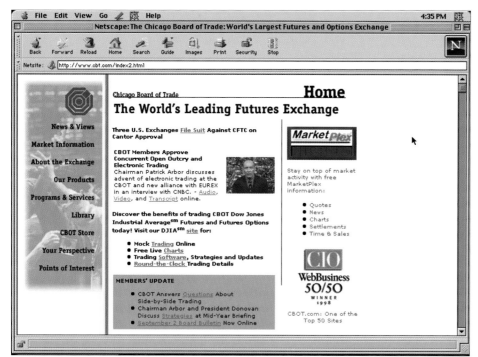

*Chicago Board of Trade*

## Other Exchanges

| | |
|---|---|
| CBOE —The Chicago Board of Options Exchange | http://www.cboe.com/ |
| Chicago Mercantile Exchange | http://www.cme.com/ |
| Chicago Board of Trade | http://www.cbt.com/ |
| | http://www.cbt.com/index2.html |
| Phildelphia Stock Exchange | http://www.phlx.com/index.stm |
| International Exchanges | http://www.doremus.com/wsn/fr_stock.html |

When moving
some things, speed
and accuracy
aren't important.

Now
let's say you're moving
50 million dollars.

In that case, there's no room for
error. We handle wire transfers
totaling over $400 billion daily.
Our commitment to technology
and customized solutions ensures
timeliness and accuracy. We let
nothing slip through our fingers.

THE
BANK OF
NEW
YORK

The
Bank of
New Ideas.

We
think
we
know
why
they're
here.

Treasury Management of a Higher Order

At AmSouth, our Treasury Management is so advanced, everyone seeks us out. That's because with our multimillion-dollar investment in cutting-edge, image-based technology, our capabilities are now light years ahead of the rest. From image disbursements and retail and wholesale lock box to windows-based information reporting and funds transfers, we can provide solutions to help you simplify management of your cash flow. No matter what the size of your business or budget. Call us today at 1-800-787-3905. You'll encounter a whole new world of Treasury Management Services.

THE RELATIONSHIP PEOPLE®

treasury@amsouth.com

## CHAPTER 7

# Risk Management

*PRUDENT RISK MANAGEMENT
first identifies the risks, then
quantifies the risk and finally
manages the risk. The treasury
manager is often charged with
managing risk as it applies
to the company's financial
assets. The Web offers treasury
managers resources on risk
management principles and
practices.* ▪

There are several contexts in which risk management applies to the treasury area. The most general context is oriented towards a company's risk relative to accidental losses. These losses will have financial implications either in terms of actual loss, or the costs incurred to control or insure against losses. In most companies this area is referred to as "insurance and risk management." Companies must also consider financial risk management as it relates to the company's financial assets. In most cases, this area of risk management involves foreign exchange, currency exposure, country risk and derivatives.

## Risk Management Terms

http://www.tmac.ca/glossry.htm

This glossary page is maintained by The Treasury Management Association of Canada.

## Fundamentals of Risk Management

http://www.contingencyanalysis.com/_x/fundamentals.htm

## Glossary of Derivatives Terms

http://www.occ.treas.gov/deriv/derivglo.htm

This page is in the Office of the Comptroller of the Currency (OCC) site and provides a glossary of derivatives terms.

## A Brief Guide to Financial Derivatives

http://www.state.pa.us/PA_Exec/Securities/corpfin/derivbro.html

This page is in the Pennsylvania State Securities Commission site and provides a basic discussion of the use and risks of financial derivatives.

## Derivatives

http://www.numa.com/index.htm

Numa Financial Systems provides a reference, index and calculators for options and warrants and links to other sites.

## Treasury Handbook

http://www.treasury.boi.ie/handbook/index.html

This site provides the user access to an online version of the *Corporate Treasury Handbook*, the essential guide for treasury risk managers. This handbook covers a wide range of treasury issues including: how to identify risks, how to go about setting a treasury policy, which derivative product to use, and when and how to structure internal controls. This handbook was written by a joint effort between Bank of Ireland and Price Waterhouse, and with its jargon free language and extensive glossary of terminology will prove invaluable to any treasury risk manager. The handbook is available in HTML form, on the web site and is also available in PDF(Portable Document Format) form, and can be downloaded in its entirety or chapter by chapter.

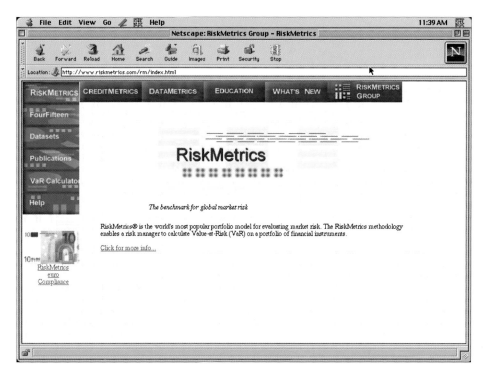

*RiskMetrics*

## RiskMetrics

http://www.riskmetrics.com/rm/index.html

This page is available from the JP Morgan site and covers their RiskMetrics® product, a methodology to estimate market risk based on the value-at-risk approach. All of the documentation (this includes a monthly printable report of benchmark volatilities and correlations) can be downloaded from this site in Acrobat™ format.

## Principles and Practices for the Oversight and Management of Financial Risk

http://www.tma-net.org/publicat/riskpub/risk2toc.html

A report from the Treasury Management Association and Ernst & Young LLP.

## Characteristics and Risks of Standardized Options

http://www.optionsclearing.com/risks/riskstoc.html

Comprehensive booklet describing standardized options prepared by The Options Clearing Corporation.

## Contingency Analysis

http://www.contingencyanalysis.com/index.htm

This is the home page for Contingency Analysis, a consulting service specializing in risk management. The site contains over 300 pages of information on financial risk management. Topics include: value at risk, derivative instruments, credit risk management and financial engineering.

# NationsBank Direct

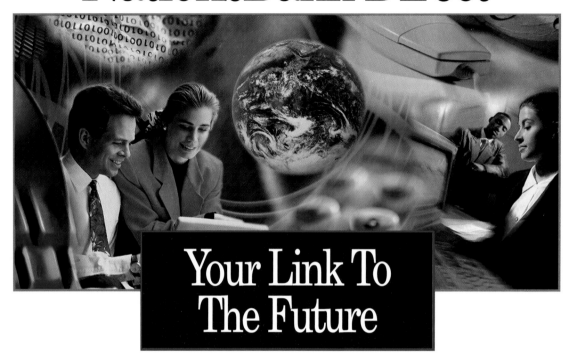

## Your Link To The Future

NationsBank Direct[sm] lets you tap the power of the Internet to manage your corporate financial activity online, real time, from your desktop.

With NationsBank Direct, you can link to the future of banking.

NationsBank Direct will feel like a direct extension of your corporate computer network — making it as easy for you to make payments or monitor lockbox receipts as it is to share a spreadsheet with a colleague down the hall.

You'll be able to move effortlessly among payments, receipts, FX, trade, investments, and borrowing activities.

NationsBank Direct will extend the range of your PC by notifying you through your pager, telephone, e-mail, fax, and more, when critical events that you designate occur.

What's more, you can bank securely knowing that we use the most advanced methods available for safeguarding electronic transactions.

Call your NationsBank Treasury Management representative today and take the first step toward a whole new way of doing business...NationsBank Direct.

**NationsBank**®

## CHAPTER 8

# Pension Management

*THE PENSION AREA HAS EVOLVED.*
*Many companies now offer their*
*employees a defined contribution*
*plan for retirement assets named*
*after the Internal Revenue Code*
*Section 401(k) that created the*
*plan. While these plans empower*
*the employees to make their own*
*investment decisions, the treasury*
*manager still has a fiduciary*
*responsibility to educate the*
*employees so they might achieve*
*retirement security. The Internet*
*can be a resource for treasury*
*managers whether their companies*
*offer a defined benefit or defined*
*contribution plan—or both.* 💻

There are a wealth of regulations and policies related to the management of employee pension funds and benefit plans. A company's pension fund generally represents a significant portion of employee compensation packages as well as a major cash flow and fiduciary responsibility. For organizations with traditional defined benefit pension plans, there is the problem of managing the plan assets to insure adequate funds will be available for employee retirements. For organizations with defined contribution plans, such as 401(k) or 403(b), management must work with the plan provider(s) to select offerings and to educate employees on using the plan.

## What is a 401(k) Plan?

http://www.kycpa.org/
Small%20Biz%20Articles/whatisa.htm

This page provides a basic discussion of 401(k) plans.

## 401(k) Plan Tips

http://www.pensionconsultant.com/
401ktips.htm

This is the site of the pension plan consulting firm, Aaron Deitsch, F.S.A. Their pension plan web site helps the user learn about pension plans, provides pension tools and applications for plans and offers help on pension plan problems. Although this pension plan site is designed for employers, it is suitable for employees, accountants, lawyers, human resource professionals and others interested in pension plans.

## Corporate Governance and Pension Plans

http://www.lens-inc.com/info/whar5.html

This page presents the results of a Wharton Impact Conference sponsored by the Pension Research Council at The Wharton School of the University of Pennsylvania. It discusses the corporate governance and pension plan administration as well as positioning pensions for the year 2000.

## Investment Manager Performance

http://www.mobiusg.com/

Möbius Group, Inc. is a provider of databases and analytical software to investment industry professionals. Their investment manager database system, M-Search, contains comprehensive qualitative and quantitative data on over 1,300 investment management firms and 5,000 companies. Möbius Group also offers over 80 broad and style-specific universes for manager peer group comparisons.

## Plan Sponsor Magazine

http://www.assetpub.com

Asset International, Inc., publishes magazines focused on institutional finance, pensions and global securities services. *The Plan Sponsor* and *Global Custodian* archives are on-line.

## Retirement Issues

http://www.ici.org/retirement/index.html

This site has a collection of articles on general issues from the Investment Company Institute.

# 401(k) Providers

| | |
|---|---|
| Aetna Retirement Services | http://www.aetna.com/financial/investment/home.htm |
| American Express Retirement Services | http://www.americanexpress.com/401k |
| AON Consulting | http://www.aon.com/prodserv/consulting/default.asp |
| Banc One Investment Management | http://www.bankone.com/corpbank |
| Charles Schwab Retirement Plan Services | http://www.schwab.com/ |
| CIGNA Retirement & Investment Services | http://www.cigna.com/retirement/index.html |
| Diversified Investment Advisors | http://www.divinvest.com/ |
| Fidelity Investments | http://www.401k.com |
| First Union | http://www.firstunion.com |
| Harris Trust & Savings Bank | http://www.harrisbank.com |
| Invesco | http://www.irps.invesco.com |
| J.P. Morgan/American Century Retirement Plans | http://www.americancentury.com |
| KeyCorp | http://www.keybank.com/business_center/corpbank |
| Loomis Sayles Funds | http://www.loomissayles.com |
| MassMutual Retirement Services | http://www.massmutual.com/ |
| Merrill Lynch | http://www.ml.com |
| MetLife | http://www.metlife.com/business |
| New York Life Benefit Services | http://www.newyorklife.com/ |
| Northern Trust Global Investments | http://www.ntrs.com |
| Prudential Investments | http://www.prudential .com |
| Putnam Investments | http://www.putnaminv.com |
| Scudder Defined Contribution Services | http://www.scudder.com |
| State Street Solutions | http://ssga.com |
| Strong Retirement Plan Services | http://www.strong-funds.com |
| T. Rowe Price Retirement Plan Services | http://www.troweprice.com |
| The Vanguard Group | http://www.vanguard.com/ |
| U.S. Bank Institutional Financial Services | http://www.usbank.com/invest/ |
| Watson Wyatt | http://www.watsonwyatt.com/401kvalue |

## Profit Sharing Council of America

http://www.psca.org

The Profit Sharing Council of America serves as a clearinghouse for private, academic and government publications about profit sharing and 401(k) plans. PSCA annually surveys hundreds of profit sharing and 401(k) plans to help its members to identify better ways to operate their own plans.

## Research — State Street Research Profile

http://www.researchmag.com/feature/a_ssr.htm

This site provides a good listing of investment and pension fund research and articles.

## Mutual Fund Center

http://www.mutualfundcenter.com/index.htm

This site is sponsored by Atlantic Financial, an independent investment firm. The Mutual Fund Center site offers information on how to select and use a mutual fund as well as frequently asked questions about mutual funds.

## Council of Institutional Investors

http://www.ciicentral.com/

The Council of Institutional Investors is an organization of large public, Taft-Hartley and corporate pension funds which seeks to address investment issues that affect the size or security of plan assets. Its objectives are to encourage member funds, as major shareholders, to take an active role in protecting plan assets and to help members increase returns on their investments as part of their fiduciary obligations.

## Investor Home — The Home Page for Investors on the Internet

http://www.investorhome.com/

Investor Home includes links and background information for each step in the investment process and all of the major asset classes including stocks, bonds, real estate, venture capital, alternative and tangible investments. The site also provides quotes and summaries of research from the industry's most respected sources as well as exclusive Investor Home features including Bulls & Bears, Who's Who in Investing (with a presence) on the Internet and Stock Market Anomalies.

## Investment Company Institute

http://www.ici.org/search.html

The Investment Company Institute sponsors this web site as part of its efforts to enhance public understanding of the investment company industry and the policy issues that affect it, particularly those involving legislation and regulation, the U.S. economy and retirement security. This page has a search engine for related articles.

## Electronic Newsletter — The 401(k) Wire

http://www.401kwire.com

The *401(k) Wire* is an on-line–based information service for professionals in the defined contribution market. The *Wire* brings timely news on the market to your desktop with an e-mail alert of stories published on-line. A free trial is available.

EDUCATIONAL CONFERENCES for organizations with pension, profit sharing, 401(k), 403(b), 457 or retirement savings plans with assets of $1 million or more.

Haas School of Business
University of California at Berkeley
MARCH 14-17, 1999
Hyatt Regency
San Francisco, CA

Stern School of Business
New York University
MAY 18-21, 1999
The Westin Hotel, Copley Place
Boston, MA

Kenan-Flagler Business School
University of North Carolina
OCTOBER 17-20, 1999
Chicago Hilton and Towers
Chicago, IL

Registration is limited *exclusively* to plan sponsors.
Outside vendors of plan services cannot enroll.

To register, or for more information, call Zoa Murray at University Conference Services at 1-800-864-2063 (8:30am-5:30pm Eastern) or visit our Web site at http://www.univconf.com

# Investment Management
## *for Institutional Investors*

*Educational Conferences for Financial Decision Makers at Pension and Retirement Plans, Foundations and Endowments*

**APRIL 20-23, 1999**
**Hyatt Regency**
**Cambridge, MA**

Presented by

**NOVEMBER 14-17, 1999**
**The Pointe Hilton**
**at Tapatio Cliffs**
**Phoenix, AZ**

Registration is limited *exclusively* to institutional investors.
Outside vendors of investment services cannot enroll.

# How To Look Smart In Today's Competitive Market.

At Mellon, we know that strong financial performance is vital to your company's image. That's why we don't give you "off-the-rack" products for your cash management needs. Instead, our industry specialists will design a comprehensive, seamless solution that looks good on you. And makes you look good to your customers. Call **1 800-424-3004** to talk to a senior advisor and visit us on the Web at **www.mellon.com** for a useful cash management idea. You won't find a better fit anywhere else.

**Mellon Global Cash Management**

## CHAPTER 9

# Seminars and Education

*FOR TREASURY MANAGERS,
keeping their knowledge base
current in a fast moving industry
is a difficult task. Fortunately,
there are many opportunities
through conferences and
continuing education events to
keep up-to-date with the changes
in the treasury management
arena. In some cases maintaining
professional certification or
accreditation may require
a minimum level of continuing
education on an ongoing basis.
This chapter tells you where
to look for educational
opportunities.* ▪

## Industry Event Calendars

*Phoenix-Hecht*
http://www.phoenixhecht.com/calendar

*Treasury Management Association*
http://www.tma-net.org/confeduc/
calendar.html

*Business Finance Magazine*
http://www.businessfinancemag.com/
index.html?CMRD=Y

*Electronic Commerce*
http://www.ecresources.com/tools/
calendar/calendar.html

## Financial Management Conferences

http://www.univconf.com/

University Conferences Services produces executive education conferences for financial, human resources and systems professionals presented in conjunction with:

Haas School of Business,
University of California at Berkeley
Kenan-Flagler Business School,
University of North Carolina-Chapel Hill
Leonard N. Stern School of Business,
New York University

### Investment Management for Institutional Investors

For financial decision makers at pension and retirement plans, foundations and endowments.

### Mid-Sized Pension Management

For organizations with pension, profit sharing, 401(k), 403(b), 457 or retirement savings plans with assets of $1 million or more.

### Financial Electronic Commerce

Formerly the Corporate EFT/ Financial EDI Conference.

### Cash and Treasury Management

Featuring two distinct tracks, Fundamentals and Advanced Topics, the programs are designed to benefit those who are new to the cash management function as well as more experienced practitioners.

## Cash Management Essentials

http://www.tma-net.org/confeduc/cme/
cmesemin.html

These seminars are offered by the Treasury Management Association in multiple locations and cover basic topics in cash management.

## Treasury Institute

http://www.tma-net.org/confeduc/ti/ti.html

A customized program in corporate finance conducted by the University of Michigan Business School in partnership with the Treasury Management Association.

## AMA Center for Management Development

http://www.amanet.org/seminars/CMD2/

The American Management Association provides educational forums worldwide. This page on the AMA site provides information on their management development seminars, many of them in the finance and treasury areas.

## Global Treasury and Financial Risk Management Short Course

http://www.intltreasurer.com/decshort.htm

This page on the site of The International Treasurer presents information on a course in the area of global treasury and financial risk management.

## IBC USA Financial Services Division

http://www.ibcusa.com/finance/index.html

IBC USA Financial Services Division produces highly focused and topical events for every sector of the financial services industry including mutual funds, capital markets, banking, insurance and pension management. Each conference addresses specific issues facing senior level professionals in marketing, product development, legal compliance, tax and accounting and more. The Financial Services Division organizes over 100 events annually.

# Appendix

# Other Index Site Links

The following index sites offer good information to treasury managers.

## Dow Jones Business Directory

http://businessdirectory.dowjones.com/

The Dow Jones Business Directory is a free service. The directory relies on technology to keep current on URL and page changes, but also on editors who continuously review new sites and analyze existing reviews.

## Financial Data Finder

http://www.cob.ohio-state.edu/dept/fin/osudata.htm

Index to financial sites maintained by the Ohio State University Fisher College of Business.

## Treasury Management

http://www.mcs.com/~tryhardz/tmp.html

Maintained by the Product Management Group ( Jim Long).

## Future Magazines

http://www.futuresmag.com/resources/fosites.html

## College of Business & Information Systems, Dakota State University, Madison, SD

http://courses.dsu.edu/finance/www/resource.htm

## On-line Reference

http://www.umi.com/

UMI, The Answer Company,™ is an information archiver and distributor offering information—via microform, paper, CD-ROM and on-line. Direct agreements with nearly 8,000 publishers and content providers enable UMI to offer information from more than 20,000 periodicals and 7,000 newspapers worldwide. Direct agreements with publishers ensure that every document is 100 percent copyright cleared. UMI is a Bell & Howell company.

## Electronic Commerce Links

http://www.ecresources.com/tools/linkpg1.html

Extensive links to Electronic Commerce sites maintained by Thomson EC Resources.

## Index to Finance Sites

http://www.gwdg.de/~ifbg/ufin.html

## Business Researcher's Interests

http://www.brint.com/interest.html

A Business Researcher's Interests is a searchable site of contemporary business, management and information technology issues. Topics include business process reengineering, knowledge management, organizational learning, complex systems and chaos, intranets, virtual corporations, outsourcing, electronic markets and electronic commerce.

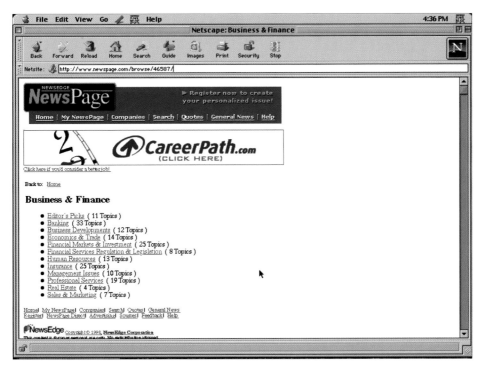

# News — Business

## Financial Services and Banking News

http://www.newspage.com/browse/46587/

NewsPage receives news from over 600 information sources every business day, filtering through thousands of news stories and keeping only the news items that are relevant to your profile. NewsEdge Corporation was formed by the merger of Desktop Data, Individual, and ADP/ISS, making NewsEdge Corporation the world's largest independent news integrator. Product offerings for the business user include free, ad-supported news on the Internet, to subscription-based services delivered on private networks. The banking and finance sources are listed below.

*American Banker*
*Bank Automation News*
*Bank Mutual Fund Report*
*Banking Attorney*
*CFO Alert*

*Corporate EFT Report*
*Credit Union Accountant*
*Document Watch*
*EFT Report*
*Electronic Claims Processing Report*
*Financial Services Report*
*International Banking Regulator*
*Item Processing Report*
*LDC Debt Report*
*NCUA Watch*
*Regulatory Compliance Watch*
*Thrift Regulator*
*Washington Watch*

### Financial Services

*Asset Sales Report*
*Bank Mutual Fund Report*
*Bond Buyer*
*California Public Finance*
*Card News*
*Comline/Japan Financial Wire*
*Credit Ratings International*

Credit Ratings in Emerging Markets
Credit Risk Management Report
Finance East Europe
Financial Regulation Report
High Yield Report
INVEST/NET Insider Trading Monitor
International Trade Finance
LDC Debt Report

Mortgage Marketplace
Pensions & Investments
Personal Policy Guide
Private Placement Report
Public Finance Watch
Securities Marketing News
The Guarantor
Treasury Manager's Report

## Other News — Business

| | |
|---|---|
| CNN Financial | http://cnnfn.com |
| The Wall Street Journal Interactive Edition | http://www.wsj.com/ |
| Financial Times | http://www.ft.com/ |
| Reuters | http://dailynews.yahoo.com/headlines/business/ |
| American Banker | http://www.americanbanker.com/ |
| Associated Press | http://wire.ap.org/?FRONTID=HOME<br>Entry to the AP News site via the Los Angeles Times or select your own local newspaper at http://wire.ap.org |
| ABC | http://www.abcnews.com |
| Business Week | http://www.businessweek.com/ |
| CBS | http://www.cbs.com |
| Forbes | http://www.forbes.com/ |
| Money Magazine | http://www.money.com |
| NBC | http://www.msnbc.com |
| NY Times | http://www.nytimes.com |
| PointCast | http://www.pointcast.com |
| PR News | http://www.prnewswire.com/ |
| Time | http://www.pathfinder.com/time/ |
| US News | http://www.usnews.com/usnews/home.htm |
| USA Today | http://www.usatoday.com |
| Wired Magazine | http://www.wired.com/news/ |

| Sports | http://home.netscape.com/bookmark/40/sportsline.html |
| | http://espnet.sportszone.com |
| | http://www.golfweb.com/ |
| | http://www.nba.com |
| | http://pathfinder.com/si/ |
| | http://www.tsn.com |
| Travel | http://www.mapquest.com/ |
| | http://www.reservations.com/ |
| | http://www.travelocity.com/ |
| | http://home.netscape.com/bookmark/40/weather.html |

# Professional Associations

There are many different associations which support treasury and cash management professional in their activities. These associations typically offer publications which keep treasury managers abreast of current issues as well as continuing education or certification to maintain the standards of the profession. Some associations also represent their members' interests to government entities or help set standards for financial transactions. Many treasurers also maintain membership in related associations, such as those for accounting, legal and investment management professions.

## Treasury Management Association

http://www.tma-net.org/

The Treasury Management Association is a national professional organization of treasury professionals. It represents more than 12,000 corporate treasury executives from 6,500 leading companies and organizations. The TMA provides many benefits to its members, including:

**Professional Development:** Annual Conference, Electronic Commerce Conference, Cash Management Essentials.

**Career Advancement and Executive Education:** Certified Cash Manager (CCM) and Certified Treasury Executive (CTE) certification program, Treasury Institute Programs.

**Technical Information/Expertise:** *TMA Journal, TMA News, Status Update of Current Issues, Electronic Commerce Report,* original research and information inquiry service, TMA's web site.

**Career Assistance:** TMA's Employment Referral Service, TMA's Jobs page.

**Other:** Representation before legislators, regulators and policy makers, discounts on publications and registrations for conferences.

## Treasury Management Association of Chicago (TMAC)

http://www.cob.niu.edu/faculty/m40wtc1/TMAC/

The Treasury Management Association of Chicago (TMAC) sponsors the annual Windy City Summit each spring in Chicago. This site contains information about TMAC's activities and its monthly newsletter.

## Treasury Management Association of New York (TMANY)

**http://www.tmany.org/**

Since its start in 1977, TMANY sponsors the New York Cash Exchange each fall and their site has their current newsletter.

## The Association of Corporate Treasurers

**http://www.corporate-treasurers.co.uk/index.html**

This web site is designed as a gateway to information on corporate treasury matters. This includes foreign exchange, interest rate, corporate finance, funding and cash management, as well as infrastructure issues like risk management, controls, treasury information systems and derivatives.

Whether you are a corporate treasurer, a banker, a finance director, a professional advisor or a government body, this web site will provide you with relevant information. It has been created by the Association of Corporate Treasurers, a UK professional body with a global outlook.

Try accessing the Technical Section for authoritative views on treasury issues and pose technical questions of current interest. Express your interest on-line in joining regional groups, becoming a member of ACT, attending conferences, furthering your education and accessing the latest treasury publications including *The Treasurer* magazine.

## Other Treasury Association Sites

**http://www.tma-net.org/library/links/assoc/regassn.html**
Contact names and addresses for local and regional Treasury Management Associations.

### Local Treasury Association Sites

| | |
|---|---|
| Dallas TMA | http://www.DallasTMA.org/ |
| Iowa TMA | http://www.wc-designs.com/itma/ |
| Minnesota TMA | http://www.mtma.com/ |
| Treasury Management Association of New England (TMANE) | http://www.tmane.org |
| Philadelphia Treasury Management Association | http://www.angelfire.com/pa/ptma/index.html |
| Treasury Association of Southern California (TASC) | http://www.tasc-la.org |
| Treasury Management Association of Western New York | http://www.tmawny.org/ |
| International Treasury Associations | http://www.tma-net.org/library/links/assoc/intlassn.html |
| Treasury Management Association of Canada (TMAC) | http://www.tmac.ca/index.html#about |

## Financial Executive Institute

http://www.fei.org/

The Financial Executive Institute is a professional organization of senior financial executives from over 8,000 corporations throughout Canada and the United States. FEI was founded in 1931 as the Controllers Institute of America, and as the responsibilities of the financial executive expanded, the Institute adopted its present name in 1962.

## NACHA — National Automated Clearing House Association

http://www.nacha.org/

The National Automated Clearing House Association (NACHA) is a not-for-profit banking trade association with the largest number of member financial institutions in the country. NACHA sets the rules and operating guidelines for electronic payments through the ACH Network, and for electronic benefits transfers, electronic checks, financial EDI and cross-border transactions.

## IFAC — Standards & Guidance — Financial and Management Accounting

http://www.ifac.org/
StandardsAndGuidance/FMAC.html

IFAC is an organization of national professional accountancy organizations that represent accountants employed in public practice, business and industry, the public sector, and education, as well as some specialized groups that interface frequently with the profession. Currently, it has member bodies in 101 countries, representing 2 million accountants.

## Association for Investment Management and Research

http://www.aimr.org/

The Association for Investment Management and Research is the leading professional organization providing global leadership for investment professionals worldwide. With over 30,000 members in more than 80 affiliated societies and chapters in over 79 countries around the world, AIMR sets the highest standards in education, ethics and advocacy for investment professionals, their employers and their clients.

## Healthcare Financial Management Association — HFMA

http://www.hfma.org/

The HFMA is the nation's leading personal membership organization for financial management professionals employed by hospitals, integrated delivery systems, long-term and ambulatory care facilities, managed care organizations, medical group practices, public accounting and consulting firms, insurance companies, government agencies and other healthcare organizations.

## American Bankers Association

http://www.aba.com/abatool/
showme_rel.html?location=homepage

The American Bankers Association represents a full spectrum of the financial services industry, including more than 90% of the nation's commercial banking assets. The ABA is a partnership of volunteer bankers and staff, dedicated to doing for its membership with their collective resources what individual bankers cannot efficiently do on their own and to enhancing the role of banks as the pre-eminent providers of financial services.

The association continues to carry forward its original missions of education, protection, self-help and government representation— while also undertaking a broad array of new, leading-edge initiatives to promote the interests of the financial services industry.

## Other Association Listings

| | |
|---|---|
| American Association of Individual Investors | http://www.aaii.org |
| American Association of Retired Persons (AARP) | http://aarp.org |
| American Bankers Association (ABA) | http://aba.com/ |
| American Bankruptcy Institute (ABI) | http://abiworld.org/ |
| American Institute of Certified Public Accountants (AICPA) | http://www.aicpa.org/index.html |
| American National Standards Institute (ANSI) | http://www.ansi.org/home.html |
| Association for Investment Management and Research (AIMR) | http://aimr.com/ |
| Bond Market Association | http://www.bondmarkets.com |
| Financial Accounting Standards Board (FASB) | http://www.rutgers.edu/Accounting/ raw/fasb/ welcome.htm |
| Financial Services Technology Consortium | http://www.fstc.org/ |
| International Organization for Standardization | http://www.iso.ch/ |
| National Association of Insurance Commissioners (NAIC) | http://www.naic.org/ |
| National Association of Credit Managers (NACM) | http://www.nacm.org/ |
| National Association of Purchasing Managers (NAPM) | http://www.napm.org/napm.html |
| National Automated Clearing House Association (NACHA) | http://www.nacha.org/index.htm |
| National Investor Relations Institute (NIRI) | http://www.niri.org/ |
| Risk and Insurance Management Society (RIMS) | http://www.rims.org/ |
| UN/EDIFACT | http://www.premenos.com/ unedifact/ |

# Government Section

There are many areas where treasury managers must interface with governments. All organizations (even the tax-exempt) must deal with the IRS and other tax entities, and any publicly-held entity must abide by SEC regulations. Many different government agencies regulate the banking industry and thus have an impact on the treasury management function of the company. Companies involved in merger or acquisition activities must also abide by the anti-trust regulations of the Department of Justice.

## Guide to Federal Reserve Regulations

http://www.ny.frb.org/pihome/regs.html

This page on the site of the New York Federal Reserve Bank contains an annotated listing of all Federal Reserve regulations.

## Uniform Commercial Code

http://www.law.cornell.edu/ucc.table.html

Latest updates to articles of the Uniform Commercial Code.

## Board of Governors of the Federal Reserve

http://www.bog.frb.fed.us/

## The Federal Web Locator

http://www.law.vill.edu/Fed-Agency/fedwebloc.html

The Federal Web Locator is a service provided by the Villanova Center for Information Law and Policy and is intended to be the one-stop shopping point for federal government information on the World Wide Web.

## Federal Reserve Bank of New York

http://www.ny.frb.org/

This site provides a wealth of information about the Federal Reserve as well as links to Internet sites for the other Federal Reserve banks.

## Other Government Sites

| | |
|---|---|
| Bureau of the Public Debt | http://www.publicdebt.treas.gov |
| Federal Deposit Insurance Corp. (FDIC) | http://fdic.gov/index.html |
| General Accounting Office (GAO) | http://www.gao.gov/ |
| GPO Gate (U.S. Govt. Printing Office) | http://ssdc.ucsd.edu/gpo |
| Office of the Comptroller of the Currency (OCC) | http://www.occ.treas.gov/ |
| Internal Revenue Service (IRS) | http://www.irs.ustreas.gov/prod/cover.html |
| Pension and Welfare Benefits Administration | http://www.dol.gov/dol/pwba |
| Securities & Exchange Commission | http://www.sec.gov/edgarhp.htm |
| Thomas (U.S. Congressional activities site) | http://www.thomas.loc.gov/home/thomas.html |
| U.S. Census Bureau | http://www.census.gov/ |
| U.S. Department of Commerce | http://www.stat-usa.gov |
| U.S. Department of Treasury — Financial Management Service | http://www.ustreas.gov/treasury/bureaus/finman/thomas.html |
| U.S. Library of Congress | http://www.loc.gov/ |
| Chicago Fed Gopher (non-Web site) | gopher://gopher.great-lakes.net:2200/11/partners/Chicago |

# Cash Management on the Web.

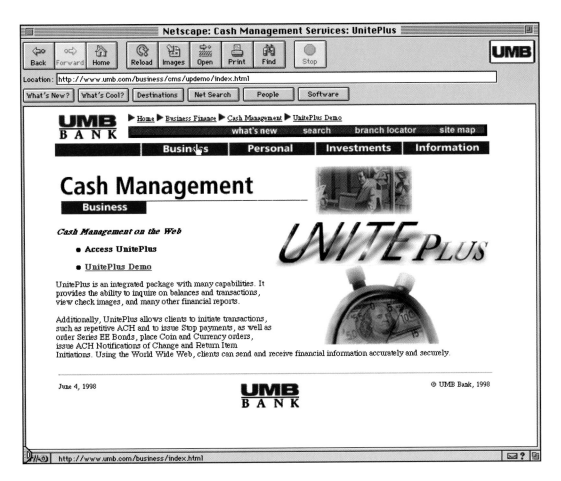

It's true with UNITE Plus from UMB Bank. Through a secure Internet browser connection, you have access to the latest account information, check images, custom reports and more. In addition, UNITE Plus incorporates the latest encryption and security techniques to safeguard data.

For more information, contact a UMB Bank Cash Management Representative at (800) 821-2171.

# UMB
# B A N K
*America's Strongest Banks*

*www.umb.com*

Missouri • Illinois • Colorado • Kansas • Oklahoma • Nebraska

www.provident-bank.com

bank

Could treasury management ever be this easy? Talk to us.

You'll deal with decision makers who can offer creative and customized

solutions tailored to your business needs. In addition, we also offer cutting

edge services like Electronic Data Interchange and our Internet Banking Service.

Call 1-800-262-9801, ext. 12088, today. **Provident Bank**

Unlike most banks, you can expect a speedy response.

# Sponsor Profiles

# AmSouth Bank

AmSouth Bank recognizes that efficiently managing cash, receivables and payables, related business expenses, and business risk are some of the toughest challenges facing companies today. It's a complex job made even tougher by changing needs and demands placed on your business such as government mandates and technological advances.

**Technology that Works** is the cornerstone of AmSouth's product offering and service delivery.

- AmSouth offers 30 years' experience in providing treasury management solutions.
- AmSouth was one of the first banks in the nation to apply imaging technology to its retail and wholesale lockbox processing.
- Its Birmingham lockbox site is continually ranked as a premier collection point for the South-Southeastern U.S. by Phoenix-Hecht.
- The bank offers image disbursement services such as positive pay and selective archival retrieval of paid checks.
- AmSouth is a leading ACH processor with a commitment to the future of EDI and multiple delivery channels needed to communicate transaction detail.

**Commitment to The Future** of treasury management is demonstrated by:

- A dedicated programming and systems group available to customize processing solutions for your company.
- A treasury management customer service hot line supported by a well-trained staff of professionals to answer your questions.
- The fact that over 60 Treasury Management Specialists and Relationship Managers have earned their CCM certification.

We deliver dependable service resulting in customer satisfaction.

**Treasury Edge**, one of our newest communication channels, can be reached through our web page using a hot link into the electronic version of this customer newsletter. In it you will find interesting articles that describe our commitment to the future . . . beyond Y2K . . . and articles that introduce new solutions for the success of your business. After all, it's a whole new world; its Treasury Management of a Higher Order.

# The Bank of New York

Founded in 1784 by Alexander Hamilton, The Bank of New York is the oldest bank in the nation operating under its original name. Today, The Bank of New York is a global financial services company and one of the largest banks in the United States, with total assets of $60 billion and offices in 26 countries.

The Bank of New York is a well-capitalized institution, with a strong balance sheet resulting from a diverse product and business mix, and a steady, experienced management team. The major credit rating agencies include the bank among the most highly rated financial institutions in the United States.

The Bank of New York offers a complete range of treasury management solutions for financial institutions, large corporations and small to mid-sized businesses. Our long-standing commitment to processing services enables us to fulfill virtually every client need.

Global financial services offered include:

- **Cash Management.** Each day we process more than 100,000 funds transfers averaging more than $400 billion. We are also among the leading providers of controlled disbursement, wholesale lockbox and local deposit services. Our information reporting capabilities are unmatched in the industry.
- **Letters of Credit.** Among the top five issuers of trade letters of credit for U.S. importers. Also, with our extensive global network of more than 2,300 correspondent banks, the Bank is a significant provider of letter of credit advising and confirmation services for U.S. exporters.
- **Securities Processing.** Domestic and global custody assets total more than $3.9 trillion. The Bank is also the market leader in U.S. Government clearance, corporate trust and global and American depository receipts, and is among the top providers of stock transfer, unit investment and master trust services.
- **Foreign Exchange.** We have a presence in significant markets around the world and offer a comprehensive array or products and consultative services. In Global Risk Management Services, we have on of the most seasoned structuring teams in the world.
- **Investment Services.** The first bank to introduce an automatic sweep from a demand deposit account to a money market fund. Today, The Bank of New York offers a full array of passive and active investment management products that may be integrated into a comprehensive treasury management solution.

## Strategically Committed to Global Treasury Management

While many banks are in the cash management business, The Bank of New York offers a unique combination of technology, products, services and expertise that allows us to deliver the treasury management solutions your company needs. We provide a complete range of treasury management services, with a dedicated focus you can only get from a bank strategically committed to transaction processing.

**Commitment.** With over 35% of the Bank's earnings derived from transaction processing services, we are dedicated to this business and have a strong incentive to continue our ongoing investment in technology.

**Customer Focus.** We coordinate our expertise across cash, custody, trade and financial market services to tailor treasury management solutions appropriate for your needs. The ongoing involvement of our sales and product management teams will help to ensure successful implementation of your treasury management system.

**Effective Operations.** Our bank-end systems employ highly sophisticated technologies that enhance our capacity to meet special customer needs. In fact, our reputation for speed, accuracy and reliability has made us one of the top three funds transfer banks in the United States.

**Advanced Technological Delivery.** On-line systems and PC-based software offer a wide array of features that deliver cash management services to your desktop. Our technology offers you flexibility, convenience and security.

**Product Breadth.** To create a comprehensive treasury management solution, we offer a complete range of cash management products that can be integrated with other services, such as investment, trade or custody activities.

## Delivery Systems: A Comprehensive Set of Options

The Bank of New York is dedicated to helping you take advantage of the latest technologies and to providing you with the greatest possible flexibility, convenience and security. With a full range of technology options, including dial-up interactive systems, network compatible software and direct CPU links, we can tailor a delivery system appropriate for your operating environment and transaction volume.

As technology moves ahead, so does our ability to offer you even easier access to banking services. In the very near future, we will offer a browser-based delivery system to provide real time, on-demand information reporting, as well as electronic payment capabilities. This system will utilize a standard industry browser, coupled with encryption and a secure token-based ID card. This security combination will provide the highest level of privacy and protection for access to your banking information.

To obtain more information about The Bank of New York's Cash Management services, please call us at (212) 815-4205 or visit us on the Internet at www.bankofny.com/cashmgmt.

# Ernst & Young LLP

Cash Management Consulting Practice
One Kansas City Place
1200 Main Street
Kansas City, MO 64105-2143

*Key Contact:*
Dave Shafer, CCM
Director
(816) 480-5436
david.shafer@ey.com

## Challenges & Changes

Increasingly, Corporate Treasurers find themselves facing new challenges. These new challenges are a result of the changing financial marketplace, corporate mergers and spin-offs, technological changes, downsizing, and the continuing consolidation in the financial services industry.

## Why Ernst & Young?

Our National Cash Management Consulting Practice can help you ensure that your cash management system is efficient and positioned to meet these new challenges, as well as give you the confidence to know that you are ready for the beginning of a new century.

Over the past two decades, Ernst & Young has helped hundreds of corporations, just like yours, establish, maintain, and improve their cash management systems. As a result of our assistance, our clients have increased their annual profitability by millions of dollars.

## Representative Sample of Industries:

- Insurance
- Manufacturing
- Mortgage Corporations
- Retail
- Utilities
- Technology/Entertainment

## Cash Management Review

A Cash Management Review (CMR) enables our clients to achieve greater profitability by increasing net interest income, reducing expenses, and improving cash management procedures and controls.

Our CMR explores all sources and uses of cash in order to ensure that we understand your organization. Based on this information, we then evaluate a variety of alternatives in order to develop recommendations that make sense for you.

## Commonly raised questions about a CMR:

**Why do I need a CMR if I don't have any problems?** Even the best system can benefit from an occasional fresh perspective. An organization is often able to receive a worthwhile recurring annual value from just a little fine-tuning.

How much time will you require of me or other personnel in my organization? We have designed our approach to the CMR to be efficient and to minimize the disruption of your day-today operations. Our consultants, not your staff, will collect and analyze the data.

## Our Commitment

We will assess the potential benefits and costs of each alternative, and determine whether a change is justified. If so, we will develop detailed and cost-effective recommendations for your consideration. As you approve the recommendations, we will work with your personnel in order to ensure timely implementation.

We want to deliver timely, quantified and implementable ideas to improve your bottom line.

# First Union

301 S. College Street
Charlotte, NC 28288
Internet: http://www.firstunion.com

*Contact:* Catherine A Bates, Vice President
Communications Director

## First Union At a Glance

With assets of $229 billion at June 30, 1998, First Union is the nation's sixth largest bank holding company. Providing financial services all along the East Coast in twelve states (Connecticut, New York, New Jersey, Pennsylvania, Delaware, Maryland, Virginia, Tennessee, North Carolina, South Carolina, Georgia and Florida) as well as Washington D.C., First Union is also the country's third largest cash management services provider, with a significant global offering.

## Global Cash Management: Solutions Through Technology

To compete in today's markets, a company must effectively use technology to control and maximize its assets. No bank in the country surpasses First Union in its commitment to helping customers navigate cash management and other financial issues unique to their business and industry. As an innovative industry leader with a strong focus on product development, First Union continually looks past conventional approaches to find creative business solutions.

First Union is recognized as a leading provider of electronic commerce, nationwide lockbox processing, Internet-based services and a variety of PC-based options. It is the only bank with all key cash management products ranked in the top ten, according to the annual Ernst & Young Cash Management Services survey. In April, 1998, **Future Banker** included First Union among its "Ten Masters of Electronic Delivery."

For nearly three decades, First Union has continually invested in technologically sophisticated products. Most recently, over $70 million has been devoted to develop products tailored to individual market segment needs over the next two years. "We are committed to being an industry leader with advanced technological capabilities and innovative product offerings," says Nina Archer, Executive Vice President and Global Cash Management Division Head. "First Union is well ahead of the curve in Year 2000 preparation so we can focus our energies and resources on bringing customers the most advanced products."

### What Sets Us Apart

Regardless of company size or industry, you can count on First Union to provide innovative solutions, proactive support and responsive service. Each relationship is managed by a trusted partner who will guide your company through today's every changing payment a processing technologies. At First Union, you will benefit from:

- Highly experienced, industry-certified consultants who work in partnership with their customers
- Product depth, interstate banking capabilities and commitment to superior operational quality
- A geographic presence that offers flexibility and a broad scope of resources
- An aggressive approach to advanced technology

First Union's Global Cash Management Division can provide you with the expertise and depth of resources you need to achieve your company's strategic growth objectives. Call us today at 1-800-377-9208. We'll listen. We'll ask questions. We'll respond.

## LaSalle National Bank

### Putting Technology to Work

LaSalle National Bank helps companies simplify, enhance and gain greater control over all facets of treasury management. By combining leading-edge technology with superior service and a worldwide network, we give clients a competitive edge.

### Secure Virtual Private Network

LaSalle is at the forefront with a suite of treasury management products that allows clients to access applications using our secure virtual private network. This innovation eliminates the need for you to maintain and upgrade the Bank's software on your system or to meet changing specification requirements. Simply dial-in to our server using a browser to obtain reporting information or initiate transactions— safely, easily and at your convenience.

### Superior Service . . .

Headquartered in downtown Chicago, LaSalle is one of the largest commercial banks in the Midwest. We have been serving businesses, institutions and individuals for more than 70 years.

### . . . Worldwide Reach

As a subsidiary of ABN AMRO Bank, LaSalle offers access to a wealth of resources for the international marketplace. ABN AMRO is a top-tier global bank with more than 1,900 locations in over 70 countries around the world, including branches in Asia, North America, South America, Europe, Africa and Australia.

## Innovative Solutions for Treasury Management

Our comprehensive services to enhance your treasury management operations include:

- **Image Technology:** View sharp digitized images of the front and back of your paid checks, invoices, purchase orders and envelopes on your screen—either on-line or by CD ROM.
- **Global Comprehensive Payables:** Send us a single electronic file of all your accounts payable, both domestic and international. Every payment is made for you—whether it's by EDI, ACH, wire transfer or check.
- **Invoice Generation:** Outsource time-consuming invoice production. Your paper invoices will be printed and mailed to your trading partners. Invoices can also be sent by fax or electronically.
- **EnhancedAR:** As cash comes in to your lockbox, we apply it to open records in your receivables database. You can dial-in to view check images and handle exceptions the same day.
- **Easy-to-Use Software:** Initiate a variety of payment transactions, retrieve and store reporting information, and initiate stop payments with CashPro+,. Our upcoming release is Year 2000 ready and will allow you to perform ACH and other transactions using your browser in a secure environment.

Take CashPro+® for a test drive. Visit www. lasallebanks.com/cashmanagement and try a free demo. We think you'll like the look, the speed and everything else about this revolutionary on-line tool that puts you in the driver's seat.

## For More Information

LaSalle's sophisticated services can simplify your treasury management operations and give you greater control. For more information, visit our web site at www.lasallebanks.com/cashmanagement or call 312/904-6815.

# Mellon Global Cash Management℠

When you select Mellon Global Cash Management (GCM) as your cash management provider, you get not only excellent products and services but also a savvy business advisor who looks at the bigger picture from your perspective. For example, when designing a solution for your company, Mellon considers the market forces that affect your industry, your company's long-term objectives, your competition and company resources.

## Take Your Treasury Office to a New Level With Mellon GCM

Whether you need a single service or a complex treasury package, there are many reasons why you should choose Mellon GCM as your cash management provider:

- A comprehensive suite of receivables, payables and treasury management solutions with service packages that fit your company's requirements.
- Innovative technology, including sophisticated security solutions for transmitting data over the Internet. Mellon is also working on numerous projects that explore the Internet's electronic commerce capabilities.
- High rankings for quality and customer satisfaction in major industry surveys.
- An ongoing consultative relationship and a commitment to customer service excellence.

It's your job to optimize your organization's financial performance. More than your typical cash management bank, Mellon GCM provides the services you want and the financial expertise you need to succeed today and in the future.

## We Can Help You Succeed

Through four decades of providing cash management services, Mellon has remained a premier performer in the financial services arena. Mellon GCM serves approximately one-quarter of U.S. businesses and institutions with annual sales of more than $500 million. These organizations, as well as our middle market customers, know that they have found a strong business partner who can help move their treasury office to a new level.

## Survey Results Confirm
## Our Strong Track Record

Mellon is one of the nation's best providers of cash management services to large corporations, according to the 1998 Phoenix-Hecht Large Corporate Cash Management Monitor Survey. Mellon's average graders in the survey's Quality Index were:

- A+ for products—customers' perceptions of timeliness, consistency and accuracy for a core group of cash management services.

- A– for marketplace perception—how customers view our capabilities in several areas such as innovation and service customization.
- B for overall sales effort—regarding the performances of GCM Sales representatives and other Mellon relationship officers.

Mellon GCM's Customer Satisfaction Survey, conducted annually by an independent research firm, found that more than 75 percent of our customers are "very satisfied" or "extremely satisfied" with their cash management relationships. The same survey revealed that Mellon is regarded as one of the most innovative banks in the country.

## Mellon Can Help You Look Your Best

To learn more about Mellon GCM and how we can help you look your best in a competitive environment, call 1-800-424-3004 or visit us on the Web at www.mellon.com.

The material presented here is intended to provide a general overview of our services and should not be construed as an offer or commitment to provide credit facilities or services. Mellon Global Cash Management is a service mark of Mellon Bank Corporation.

# NationsBank

NationsBank Corporation is a top provider of services and information to help businesses, financial institutions and government agencies effectively manage their financial activities -- both domestically and internationally.

NationsBank leads the Treasury Management industry in developing and delivering emerging technologies that help companies increase the efficiency of their payments, receipts, and treasury operations.

At NationsBank, we combine decades of Treasury Management expertise with our extensive interstate banking operations, to deliver comprehensive, nationwide solutions to our customers' business needs.

## Developing New Banking Tools
## For A New Business Era

NationsBank is at the forefront of developing new banking tools for a new business era. We invest in new technology and in the creative minds that understand its potential, building on simple – yet powerful – principles.

- **Information Is Power**

  NationsBank is committed to getting you the information you need, when you need it, in a format you can use—empowering you to get the job done.

- **Technological Tools Can Break Down Barriers**

  By employing the technology that's becoming the standard for our times, NationsBank helps you break down the barriers of time and geography so you can more efficiently manage your business.

- **Take A Fresh Approach To Technology**

  NationsBank uses state-of-the-art tools to give you maximum control over the way you interact with NationsBank and the way NationsBank interacts with you. Whether we're introducing groundbreaking capabilities that empower you to designate the important events you want NationsBank to notify you of as soon as they happen, or incorporating rules-based logic in our systems so you can "teach" NationsBank applications to work the way you do, we're taking a fresh approach to technology that's become a NationsBank hallmark.

- **Security For Your Peace Of Mind**

  NationsBank understands the importance of security in all banking transactions. We employ extensive security in our banking networks to deliver a dependable, secure environment – and peace of mind for our customers.

### Link To The Future With NationsBank

NationsBank is the technology leader in the banking industry, committed to developing innovative solutions to our customers' business challenges. Call your NationsBank Treasury Management representative today, or visit our website at www.nationsbank.com, and link to the future with NationsBank.

## PNC Bank

PNC Bank Corp. was created by the 1983 merger of Pittsburgh National Corp. and Provident National Corp. PNC Bank Corp., headquartered in Pittsburgh, is listed on the New York Stock Exchange; its ticker symbol is PNC.

### Treasury Management

Effective management of your company's cash flow is one of the most critical factors to ensuring the success of your business. PNC Bank's national leadership in treasury management services helps you keep your cash working, 24 hours a day, 7 days a week:

- PNC Bank offers a full range of treasury management services both domestically and globally with a focus on exceeding our client's needs.

- We employ the most knowledgeable and skilled treasury services professionals and empower them to satisfy your unique business and systems requirements.
- Improving your productivity and profitability is what we're all about.
- We are an industry leader in every significant measure of financial strength.

### Vision Statement

- We are dedicated to providing the highest quality service as the treasury management bank of choice by a growing base of satisfied clients.
- Our mission is to improve our client's productivity and profitability. We innovate and customize our products to improve client

processes and deliver more cost effective solutions.

## Business Mission

- **Reputation for Innovation**

  Known in our markets as the leader of choice for innovative solutions.

- **Highest Quality Service Delivery**

  Earn the confidence of our clients by exceeding their expectations with products and service.

- **Fastest Growing Among Our Peers**

  Achieve a sustaining edge among our competition through managed growth, application of technology and ongoing reinvestment.

- **First Position in Footprint—Top Five Nationally**

  Be the treasury management bank of choice in our franchise and in the top five in national providers.

## Electronic Commerce

PNC Bank's commitment to client satisfaction is evidenced by our continuing efforts to deliver comprehensive business solutions over multiple delivery channels. The Internet represents the newest medium over which PNC Bank is working to offer its broad array of products and services. PNC Bank is dedicated to leveraging the Internet opportunity through strategic alliances, consortiums and internal development.

Put the power of our performance to work for your company through our integrated collection solutions, disbursement solutions, information management solutions and investment management solutions.

## The Provident Bank

www.provident-bank.com
1 East Fourth Street
Cincinnati, Ohio 45202

The Provident Bank is a subsidiary of Provident Financial Group, Inc. (NASDAQ: PFGI), a Cincinnati-based commercial banking and financial services company with managed assets of $9.5 billion that provides full service regional banking and brokerage operations in Ohio, Kentucky and Florida.

Provident Bank is a leader in providing businesses with innovative and automated banking services. Provident's commercial products and services can provide your business access to the type of financial information necessary to make critical decisions about managing cash flow, reconciling accounts and investing surplus funds.

### PROCASH^SM Internet Connection

- Cash Management Services available 24 hours-a-day directly through the Internet
- Previous day and current day balance reporting
- Stop Payment initiation and bank statement printing available
- Security provided through the latest encryption technology, which also accommodates a large number of users simultaneously

### PROCASHSM PROEDI for the Internet

- Use a standard web browser
- Initiate all types of payments including check,

wire and financial EDI payments

- Receive payment and remittance acknowledgments online

## PROCASH*SM* Electronic Bank Window

- Retrieve current, previous and historical account information.
- Access information through various networks or stand alone PC's.
- Initiate Stop Payments
- Generate outgoing wire transfers and provide detail of incoming wire transfers on an intraday basis.
- Originate ACH transactions.

With the proper combination of innovative Cash Management Services from Provident Bank, your company can monitor and control funds with a higher degree of accuracy, make decisions with greater confidence and ultimately increase profitability.

For more information, please contact our Corporate Services Department:

Jerry Meyer, Vice President
(513) 579-2347
jmeyer@provident-bank.com

Jim Hamberg, Vice President
(513) 579-2619
jhamberg@provident-bank.com

Dave King, Vice President
(513) 639-4725
dking@provident-bank.com

## Provident Bank Corporate Services' Focus

Our mission is to provide the highest quality products and services designed to meet the needs of the corporate market with a variety of customized and innovative banking solutions.

# SunGard Treasury Systems*SM*

## Who We Are

SunGard Treasury Systems (STS) is the new force in the global treasury and risk management software industry. With an installation base of 500+ companies worldwide including 50 of the fortune 100 domestic companies, STS is the largest player in a very large market. For the first time ever, a company in the corporate treasury risk management arena has reached the critical mass necessary to fully develop the expanding ranges of technological options and apply them to the goal of global treasury management.

## Where We Came From

STS was formed in 1998 as a new business unit of the SunGard Trading Systems Group by combining the operations of Multinational Computer Models (MCM) and the ResourceIQ product line of ADS Associates. The formation of STS has created the largest team of treasury industry experts solely focused on the development and support of global treasury and risk management systems.

## Our Goal

Our goal is to be the premier provider of integrated treasury management solutions. By focusing on the critical components of a fully integrated treasury operation, we have assembled the most comprehensive suite of products in the industry. We offer treasury managers an end-to-end solution, covering everything from cash management and financial planning to forecast to trading and risk management systems. We offer front, middle, and back office products that can accommodate everything from domestic cash management operation to a multinational and real time trading environment.

## Work Flow Management

Our approach to systems management is to provide the critical components of **Transactions Processing, Operations Control, Connectivity,** and **Decision Support** within an environment of **Workflow Management.** Where other vendors have specialized in one or two of these areas, SunGard Treasury Systems has the resources to provide the complete solution. The focus on Workflow Management insures that each of the critical components are brought together in an integrated and intuitive fashion.

## Where We Are Going

The dramatic growth in volume of financial transactions and the complexity and diversity of financial alternatives to the corporate treasurer has created the need for a global strategic partner. With offices around the world and the most experienced and knowledgeable professional staff in the industry, SunGard Treasury Systems is ready to be your partner.

# SunTrust Banks, Inc.

SunTrust began operation on July 1, 1985, as a regional bank holding company based in Atlanta, Georgia. It was formed by the merger of Trust Company Banks of Georgia, which was founded in 1891, and SunBanks of Florida, with a history dating back to 1934. In July of 1998, SunTrust signed a definitive agreement to acquire Crestar Financial Corp., based in Richmond, Virginia. The completion of this acquisition will make SunTrust a regional superpower with a presence in six Southern states and the District of Columbia. SunTrust assets totaled $62 billion at the time of the merger announcement and with the acquisition of Crestar, total assets are estimated to total approximately $88 billion, making SunTrust the nation's 10th largest bank.

SunTrust provides a wide range of corporate, institutional and personal financial services, including traditional banking services, trust and investment management, investment banking, factoring, international, credit cards, treasury management and leasing services. SunTrust owns 48.3 million shares of common stock in The Coca-Cola Company, which were obtained when SunTrust served as an underwriter for Coke's initial public offering in 1919.

*Any Bank Can Offer Treasury Management Products, But SunTrust Has The Talent It Takes To Design Creative Solutions.*

*Every dollar of your company's cash should be working hard for you,* from the moment it is available to the time it's spent. Standard products alone may not help you achieve that goal, but a partnership with SunTrust can.

*We understand that effective treasury management is a creative process* with endless possibilities for managing the flow of cash into accounts, controlling disbursements, generating additional interest income, increasing working capital and efficiently using your internal resources.

*That's why SunTrust professionals will help you develop innovative treasury management solutions* that meet your needs. Then fine-tune them as your company grows and changes.

*SunTrust has assembled all the key elements for successful treasury management,* including innovative services, quality delivery of those service, leading edge technology and the resources and commitment of one of the top banks in the nation.

*But what really sets us apart is our people.* We actively seek out and employ treasury management professionals who have the problem-solving abilities and the financial ingenuity it takes to help you develop the best solution for your company.

### Our Professionals Will Analyze Your Company's Situation—And Develop High-Performance Solutions.

*At SunTrust, we focus on long-term relationships.* That means building a solid foundation from the very beginning.

*Our professionals work closely with you* to understand your company's unique financial position and goals. Then they combine a thorough knowledge of treasury management principles with creative thinking and advance technology to come up with solutions that help you meet your business objectives.

*Your SunTrust team will keep you informed* on the latest technology, industry trends and new ways to optimize your treasury management process—including ideas that are being used successfully by other companies.

### The Result of Our Innovative Thinking: Some Of The Most Advanced Services Available Anywhere.

*In the process of developing tailored operating solutions for our corporate clients,* SunTrust has become an industry leader in a number of key areas.

*For example,* we are well known for our work in employing image technology. We're highly skilled in providing electronic bank window and systems integration. And we offer a full range of electronic commerce services.

*Our treasury management professionals* have helped many top companies re-engineer their financial systems. Your company can benefit from that experience and from our substantial technological investment.

### With SunTrust Treasury Management Service, Today's Solutions Are Just The Beginning.

*When your business changes,* so do your treasury management needs. As your long-term partner, we'll be there to fine-tune your systems for peak performance.

*We place great importance on creating* and maintaining a strong working relationship with your company.

*It's just what you'd expect from SunTrust,* a bank that was built on responsive service and is now one of the largest banking organizations in the United States.

*With this kind of commitment,* it's no surprise that SunTrust has achieved a high satisfaction level among clients, as evidenced by consistently high independent survey scores and by our own client "report cards."

*If you're interested in getting the most from every corporate dollar, come to SunTrust.* We have tailored treasury management solutions for hundreds of companies across the country. And we welcome the opportunity to put our talent and resources to work for you.

# UMB Financial Corporation

UMB Financial Corporation is a regional, multi-bank holding company headquarted in Kansas City, Missouri. The Company, with $7.1 billion in assets, offers complete banking and related financial services to both individual and business customers, including employee benefit services, trust and estate planning, cash management, financial counseling, brokerage services and commercial loans.

The Company owns and operates 16 affiliate banks with nearly 160 locations throughout Missouri, Illinois, Kansas, Oklahoma, Nebraska and Colorado. All banks are recognized by the UMB initials. Subsidiaries of the holding company and the lead bank, UMB Bank, N.A., include a corporate trust and securities processing company in New York, a trust employee benefit office in San Francisco, a trust management company in South Dakota and single-purpose companies that deal with brokerage services, leasing, venture capital and insurance.

For more information about UMB Bank's Cash Management Services call 1-800-821-2171. Other key contacts include Timothy M. Connealy, Chief Financial Officer and David D. Miller, Executive Vice President and Corporate Secretary.

In Missouri: 800-892-2434.

# Union Bank of California

Everyone talks about technology. And Union Bank of California's technological innovations like CLEAR/IMAGE Hindsight$^{SM}$ offer our customers important cutting-edge benefits to help them compete in today's market. But even the best technology needs a human element to make it a reality.

By combining the speed and convenience of our up-to-the-minute technology with highly personalized service, Union Bank of California helps you operate more efficiently, optimize your cash flow and improve your bottom line.

## At the Forefront of Technology

Union Bank of California's commitment to technological and financial innovations offers you the ability to monitor and control your finances more easily than ever before. We'll support you with state-of-the-art banking technology, including installation of software, training for your staff and ongoing technical support.

We're turning today's technology into convenient banking services:

- Complete check image capabilities on-line—Union Bank of California was one of the first banks to offer the service.
- Financial Electronic Data Interchange capabilities, including the ability to make and receive ANSI 820, ANSI 835 and custom-formatted electronic payments.
- Sacramento County this summer became the first county in California to make its General Assistance benefits available through electronic transfer services provided by Union Bank of California.

## Customized Personal Service

Union Bank of California received overall A ratings for General Perception and Relationship Managers in the 1998 Phoenix-Hecht market survey. These ratings reflect our reputation for expertise and customer service—hallmarks at Union Bank of California since its founding in 1864.

The key difference Union Bank of California offers is really knowing a company and its industry. Our relationship managers specialize in select industries in order to understand the needs, trends and special requirements of the customers in the segments they serve, including:

- Communications/Media
- Financial Institutions
- Retailing Industry
- Real Estate Industries
- Financial Services Industries
- Entertainment
- Government
- Health Care
- Utilities
- Oil and Gas

### Strength and Stability

Union Bank of California is the third-largest commercial bank in California and is among the 30 largest banks in the United States, based on Second Quarter 1998 assets of $29.8 billion. UBOC has 241 branches in California, three branches in Washington, two in Oregon, and offices in New York and Texas, as well as 18 international offices, principally along the Pacific Rim.

Union Bank of California
445 South Figueroa Street
Los Angeles, CA 90017
http://www.uboc.com

*Key contact:*
JoAnn Bourne, Senior Vice President
213.236.7901

## Wachovia

### Wachovia Offers Electronic Commerce Solutions

Among the nation's financial services institutions, Wachovia is an acclaimed leader with a long-standing reputation for the scope and caliber of its services . . . its leadership in developing innovative uses of technology . . . and its standing as one of the soundest and most respected financial institutions in the world, with the resources to continue making solid investments in new products and technology.

Wachovia's strengths include cash management expertise and emphasis on operational excellence, supplemented by alliances worldwide to provide seamless service delivery. Independent national studies laud Wachovia's relationship approach to serving customers' needs. In a quest for innovative solutions, Wachovia's corporate specialists work closely with each company to gain a thorough understanding of its treasury management needs, from traditional domestic cash management to global treasury services.

Wachovia has a strong commitment to developing and enhancing Electronic Commerce solutions for commercial customers—enabling them to manage costs, streamline processing and use staff efficiently while still controlling check fraud, meeting corporate and consumer payment requirements, minimizing exception processing and manual procedures, and planning for contingencies.

Solutions such as Integrated Payables, imaging for disbursements and collections, and commercial card programs provide flexibility, security and quality service from a committed partner. Drawing on more than 20 years of experience as a leader in electronic payment services, Wachovia has streamlined the payments process through a combination of services that increase productivity and while providing access to sound, technologically advanced capabilities.

From consulting to system design to daily implementation, Wachovia's focus is on practical solutions tailored to each company's needs. It is this approach—and proven expertise—that for more than a century has earned Wachovia a solid position of leadership in an increasingly complex, global and discerning market.

To learn more about Electronic Commerce solutions, call Wachovia at 1-800-422-4950 or visit our web site at www.wachovia.com.

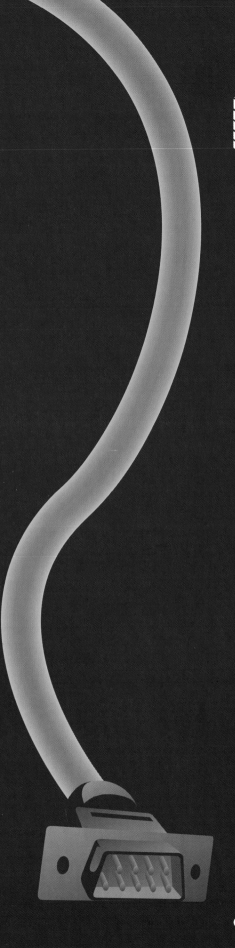

THE 12TH ANNUAL

# FINANCIAL ELECTRONIC COMMERCE

## CONFERENCE

## April 6-9, 1999
## Chicago Hilton and Towers

An Executive Education Program
for Financial and Systems Executives
and EDI/EC Team Members

### PRESENTED BY

*95% of Past Participants Would
Recommend this Conference to a Peer*

### SPONSORED BY

ABN-AMRO/LaSalle National Bank
Bank of America
First Chicago NBD
First Union National Bank
Harris Bank/Bank of Montreal
Mellon Global Cash Management[SM]
National City
PricewaterhouseCoopers
SunTrust Banks, Inc.
Thomson EC Resources
Union Bank of California
U.S. Bank
Visa U.S.A.
Wachovia Corporation

**To register, or for more information, call Zoa Murray
at University Conference Services at 1-800-864-2063
(8:30am-5:30pm Eastern) or visit our Web site
at http://www.univconf.com**